REDEMPTION

"From the Crack House to God's House"

Bethann Codrington

REHOBOTH
— PUBLISHING, LLC —

"Crack cocaine is a smoked version of cocaine that provides a short, but extremely intense, high. It's one of the most psychologically addicting drugs"

Preface

The majority of my adult life was over-shadowed by violence, crime and prostitution, which was all fueled by my fierce battle with a more than 30-year crack cocaine habit. Each year got progressively worse. My life had spiraled completely out of control, down into a horrible pit of living hell. I was travelling on a fast moving train of death, destruction and eternal damnation. Only God could save me from myself and stop the inevitable.

Then one day, with a truly repenting heart, I cried out to the Lord to save and deliver me. He heard my prayer and by His grace, snatched me out of the jaws of despair. It was there in my deliverance I found out that God always had a plan for my life. Now, everywhere I go, I give my personal testimony declaring the miracle healing and delivering power of Jesus Christ. Part of my personal mission is to let the world know that if He can deliver me out of all of the mess and mire that bound me for decades, anyone can be delivered. In my witnessing, especially to addicts, I share the gospel of John 8:36 that says, *"Whom the Son sets free is free indeed."*

When I share my testimony, I speak realness because although I am free from the stranglehold of addiction and have been redeemed, I am not free from the damage I caused which was profound. I caused a lot of pain and inflicted horror upon my family and friends. I did a lot of dirt, which left a trail of un-repairable relationships and a host of enemies, some of whom wish death upon me. To be perfectly blunt, I burned every single bridge possible. Some people I hurt to their core and they still harbor genuine hate for me. Honestly, I can't say I blame them. They question my motives and my declaration of freedom from bondage. Most of them believe I'm still that lying and deceiving Bethann who is off to her next scam, the church hustle. I get it though, because I was a savage who did any and everything to any and everybody to get what I wanted. The constant pursuit and use of crack took all my pride, decency and integrity. But thanks be to God, the story didn't end there. I am blessed. I had people who never gave up on me and believed that in spite of all my flaws and chaos God had a plan for me. Contrary to what most people believed, everyone had not given up on me. More importantly, the person who mattered the most, God, had not turned His back on me. I also had a praying mother who believed that prayer changed things. And she believed God's word that *"The effectual fervent prayers of the righteous availeth much."* In addition, God had dispatched a set of twins, "Goodness and Mercy," that were by my side to protect me. Now it's important that I make it clear, although He protected me, I still went through hell. I was beaten up, robbed, raped and sodomized. The devil did everything he could to try and kill me. But in spite of all the dysfunction and craziness of my life, God never left me. The psalmist let me know if I make my bed in hell God would be there. He was and He came and got me.

Now instead of someone else writing a sad eulogy about my wasted, drug-addicted life, I am alive to write the story of my redemption and the power and victory in Jesus Christ. Also, I have established a ministry called, "Finding Hope in God," to help give hope to the hopeless.

All along my journey, God put people in my life that helped protect me and keep the death angel away. I may not mention you by name in the book, but please know that I thank you, I pray for you and I will never forget you.

Dedication

This book is dedicated to the life and the memory of my late mother, Charlene Strother, the matriarch and chief encourager of my family. My mother was an amazing woman with a giant heart. To know her was to love her. She made a lasting impact on all she came in contact with. Her love of God was infectious, sincere and pure. Quite simply, she believed God was the answer to everything. Now, I won't try and paint her as Mother Teresa or some perfect person because no man is good or free from sin. In fact, Jesus Himself, in the Book of St. Mark, Chapter 8 said, *"None is good but the Father."* My mother had her struggles just like every other person born of flesh. However, she didn't allow those struggles to separate her from the love of God. Instead, she used her love and commitment to God and her undying faith in His Holy Word to weather the storms of life. God was her first love, but her children were a very close second. Each of her children were special and important to her in our own way. She had an unbreakable bond and never-ending dedication to us all. Notwithstanding, in life your kids don't always turn out the way you plan and prepare for them. Sometimes they make poor choices that result in awkward, challenging and compromising situations. But regardless of the bad decisions we made and the hurt and disappointment we may have caused her, she kept on praying.

The black cloud that my drug addiction had over the family and all the destruction that came with it wasn't strong enough to separate us. And, in spite of all the torment, heartache and pain I caused, her faith assured her that God had a greater plan for my life. She stood steadfast in prayer and supplication for my deliverance. Even when my family, friends and church members told her I was a lost cause and to cut me loose, she kept on praying and believing God for my deliverance. She never gave up on me.

On February 17, 2010, after my 30 plus years of battling drug addiction, my mother's prayers were answered and the Lord saved me. I walked into church and the Lord transformed me from an unrepenting crackhead to a saint of God. And then a few short months later on May 29, 2010, God completely delivered me from the taste of drugs, just as my mother believed He would. I have never touched a drug or alcohol since that day.

My mother went on to be with the Lord before she could witness her answered prayers for my deliverance. However, I believe she is looking down from heaven, cheering me on to the finish line. The Word of God in the 12th chapter of the Book of Hebrews says: *"Wherefore seeing we also are compassed about with so great a cloud of witnesses, let us lay aside every weight, and the sin which doth so easily beset us, and let us run with patience the race that is set before us."* God blessed me with my angel, Charlene, and because of her faith, love and prayers, I am saved and working daily to help others overcome addiction and to win souls for the Kingdom of God. This book is a testimony of a mother's love for her child and the healing and delivering power of the Almighty God.

Introduction

"For I know the plans I have for you," declares
the Lord, "plans to prosper you and not to harm
you, plans to give you hope and a future."
Jeremiah 29:11

God has a unique plan for His people. Before the foundation of the world, He ordained a purpose and a plan for us. He put this plan in his Word. The scriptures let us know that God's plan is for us to prosper, be free from harm and to give us hope. What the world needs today is more hope—hope in the future, hope in the resurrection and hope in the soon-coming Savior. My main goal and purpose for writing this book is to offer you that hope which saved me and changed my life. Follow me as I share my life experiences on the road to my redemption. For many years, just like a lot of you, I lived way beneath my privilege, mostly because of sin and disobedience. Before I accepted Christ, everything about my life was contrary to God. Be advised sin and disobedience will always lead you out of fellowship and away from God. My actions and choices took me away from God into a living hell. But the prayers of the righteous, mainly my mother's, along with the help of twins, "Goodness and Mercy," kept me alive to experience my miraculous transformation. Please believe that what God did for me is truly a miracle. When you have truly been chosen, such as I have been, God will always make provisions on your behalf.

See, for more than 30 years, I was a drug addict. I abused all kinds of pills, alcohol, marijuana, heroin and crack cocaine. I was one of the biggest crackheads in Boston. During my time of getting high, I'll bet I smoked up close to a million dollars' worth of cocaine. I'm not bragging or glorifying what I did, but I need you to understand the extent of my addiction. I was a queen crackhead and that's no title that I'm proud to have. But it's just the cold hard facts. I use the word "crackhead" to remind me where I came from and how the Lord delivered me. There was nothing glamorous or exciting about that lifestyle. It was a nasty, disgusting life that only brought emptiness, hurt and shame to me and my loved ones. Some people, especially those actively using crack, may not like my use of the word, crackhead, but I don't want to downplay or minimize what and who I was before God changed my life.

During the time of my active drug use, I was a complete reprobate. I committed all kinds of crimes, including robbery, fraud and prostitution. And although I was aware and hated who I was, I couldn't stop. Nobody was safe on the streets if I caught them slippin', especially if I was really feigning. To keep it all the way real or as the kids say, "Keep it 100," I was a crazy, basehead, crackhead, drug fiend that terrorized my family, the community and anyone in my trail on my pursuit of drugs. Nothing and no one could out-think, out-hustle or out-con me when it came to getting high. Not too many people had a habit like mine or pulled the type of sophisticated scams that I did. To those who knew me back then I was a lost cause, just a hopeless addict. No one from my past life would ever think that God could clean me up, redeem me and take me from the crack house to His house. When people from back in the day see me today, they can't believe I'm the same person. They are partially right. I'm still Bethann, but like 2nd Corinthians 5:17 says: *"Therefore, if any man is in Christ, he is a new creature: old things have passed away; behold, all things have become new."* I'm a new creation, and God has work for me to do. The old saints used to say, *"God's got a job that only you can do."* And they would also let you know that "your gift would make room for you."

Having been elevated to a new level in God, I understand everything they were saying. Some readers might say, "Why would God want to use an ex-crackhead?" But if you read the Word of God, you will see that some of the greatest people in the Bible had significant character flaws and some lived horrible lives before coming to Christ. For example, Noah was a drunk, and God used him. Rahab was a prostitute, God used her. King David was an adulterer and murderer, and God used him. And now it's my turn. Bethann, the former crackhead, stealing, prostituting sinner, has a work to do, and God has chosen to use me.

Chapter One

"For many are called, but few are chosen."
St. Matthew 22:14

Having been chosen by God and plucked out of hell's fire, it's important that my life be in complete order as I represent the Kingdom of God. I have to be a living example of the power of God that set me free from the bondage of drug addiction and sexual immorality. Therefore, my days of being slick and taking shortcuts are long gone. Besides, I know I can't be an effective witness for Christ if I'm on the fence and still doing some of the things I profess the Lord delivered me from. I'm aware I have eyes all over me. The church world is watching, the streets are watching, my family is watching and, most importantly, God is watching. If I compromise myself, then I'm nothing more than a hypocrite unfit for the Kingdom, and the world has more than enough of those. Not to brag, because I make my boast in the Lord, but that can never be an option for me. Even when I was smoking crack every day, I wasn't a hypocrite. So if I can go all out for the world, I can go all out for Jesus.

As I said earlier, God has an assignment for each of us. However, we can't understand the true destiny or the divine assignment He has for us unless Jesus reveals it. We can dream, set goals and have visions, but in order for any of our plans to prosper, they must line up with the will of God. Often, I dream about things I want to do for the Lord because I'm so grateful for all He has done for me. I have big plans and bigger ideas. There are so many things I want to do for God's people, especially the lost ones who can't see their way out of bondage. But in my mission to glorify God, I have to make sure that "self" is put on the back burner because "self" always wants to be seen and "self" always leads to trouble. There is an old saying that the road to hell is paved with good intentions. Motives are important. I asked God to keep me humble and keep my motives pure. If your motives are out of whack, you will find yourself doing things contrary to God and eventually find yourself out of fellowship. The old folks had a saying that "You don't backslide overnight, it's a gradual process."

As I continue to develop in my ministry and service of the Lord, I see more and more how "self" can lead to negative outcomes and sometimes lead you out of the will of God. "Self" is a powerful being. In my years in and around church, I have seen a lot of people who wanted to preach but had not been called. Some of them were gifted and really talented, while others just had zeal, but it was not according to knowledge. There were also others who declared themselves prophets and wanted to prophesy. They loved telling you what "Thus saith the Lord" or what the Lord was going to do for you in 30 days. And even though sometimes those things they spoke of came true, some of those men and women were not truly chosen. They are exposed sooner or later when what they said was going to happen never occurs. But the reality is that many of these people have talents and gifts. Just be mindful of what the Apostle Paul wrote about these

16

people in Romans 11:29, *"For the gifts and calling of God are without repentance."* Over the years, I've seen that scripture come to life. I have witnessed first-hand people whom I know, beyond the shadow of a doubt, not living the life they were preaching about. I'm talking about pimps in the pulpit pretending to be pastors. Some of these men and women are master entertainers. They know how to get the congregation pumped up. Some can even preach the Kingdom down. They could lead people to Christ and even help them get delivered. And if you don't have a discerning spirit, you might think they were legit, but they are not the real thing.

Some of those same so-called men and women of God who had the church in a "praise frenzy" were living "down-low" and had secret lives. By day, they were upstanding people of the community appearing to bring forth the Word of God with conviction and authority; and by night, they were on the stroll looking for sex. How do I know this you might ask? Because I was out in those same streets and saw them. But how do I really and truly know? I know because I tricked with a few of them. For those of you not sure what "tricked" is, it means I had sexual relationships with some of them while I was out prostituting. Actually referring to our encounters as sexual relationships doesn't make it sound so bad. So let's just say I screwed them for money. That may sound vulgar to some of you reading and I don't want to offend you. But I need you to understand the realness of what goes down in those streets. So when I see any of those "tricks" and they are getting up in front of a congregation acting holier than thou and talking about holiness and righteousness, I chuckle to myself. And then when they have the audacity to talk about the "sanctity of marriage" I sometimes roll my eyes, suck my teeth and shake my head. There was nothing sanctified about you and me having unprotected sex in your Cadillac Escalade in the back alley on Blue Hill Ave. at 3:00 in the morning. You were not witnessing to me. We were not studying scripture and the only time you were speaking in tongues was when you were climaxing. I haven't exposed them yet, but if they don't change I may name names in my next book. However, right now I just pray for them. And while their ways disgust me, they helped me come into the realization of why my mother would always say, "Puncho, you have to know Jesus for yourself."

Chapter Two

"You need to know God for yourself."
Mother Charlene Strother

Each year as I get older I see more and more how anointed my mother really was. I see how her love of the scriptures and dedication to prayer and studying benefitted me. She always presented Christ to me no matter my condition. It didn't matter if I was high or sober; she always had a word for me. One of the scriptures she quoted often is found in the Book of Romans: *"And we know that all things work together for good to them that love God, and to them who are the called according to his purpose."* It's actually one of the most quoted scriptures in the church and I've probably heard it quoted more than 100 times in my life. But it wasn't until I was completely delivered from crack cocaine and the craziness of my past lifestyle that I really understood it. That is because it used to be hard to believe anything good could come out of the trauma and tragedies that occurred in my life. How in the world could incest, rape, physical and sexual abuse and crack addiction ever work for my good?

However, as a born again, Holy Ghost filled believer, working to help inspire hope to the lost, I have a better understanding that "ALL" things means "ALL" things! Because of all my crazy experiences, I am able to share with people my life of addiction and how I was delivered. In the process, I let them know the good things we experience, the bad things we endure, the highs of life, and the lows too, the ups as well as the downs, together they make up the "ALL" things, that work together that Apostle Paul was talking about in his letter. In order for you to truly understand the deepness of that scripture, you must develop an intimate relationship with God. It's not enough to just go to church. There are people who go to church every week and still don't have a real intimacy with God. You have to love God and love spending quality time conversing and fellowshipping with Him. You need to develop a level of closeness that is deeper than any natural friendship and stronger than any bond, even that between a husband and wife. It's a closeness that causes you to say as Apostle Paul said in Philippians 3:10: *"I want to know Christ and experience the mighty power that raised Him from the dead. I want to suffer with Him, sharing in His death."* That's another powerful passage of scripture that points you to a level of intimacy that can only be attained with a loving God. If I were to break down the essence of that scripture to the younger generation, that's easier to understand, I would say Jesus needs to be your "ride or die" because that's what He became for us when He made the ultimate sacrifice at Calvary. I heard someone say "He was hung-up for our hang-ups." That's all the crazy, risky and sometimes stupid stuff we do. It also includes the mental illness, sickness and diseases we battle. He was crucified for it all. He paid the ultimate price for each of us.

In my case, He did it knowing one night I would get so out-of-my-mind high on crack and do the unthinkable and have unprotected sex with a man who had full blown AIDS. I'm talking about a man who was sick and dying, due to AIDS. A man who looked like death had already taken ahold of him. With all the warnings and red flags that were telling me to run the other way, my addiction convinced me to lay down with him. Because he wanted it raw, we didn't use a condom. No person in their right mind would do such a crazy thing. But I was a deranged, crack fiend, willing to die for that next hit. I was so strung out that I continued to have sex with that same infected man a few more times, playing a dangerous game of Russian Roulette with my life, until his money ran out. Then I was on to the next trick. At that time, AIDS was considered a death sentence. People stayed far away from those infected because they were so scared of even touching someone with AIDS, never mind having unprotected, sexual intercourse with them, as I did. But in the moment of chasing that high it didn't matter to me, it was worth the chance

Thank God He was faithful to me even when I wasn't faithful to myself. Whenever I give my testimony, I always say God assigned the twins, "Goodness and Mercy," to protect me. This is especially true on the night a Boston policeman, one of Boston's finest, ran up on me and made me strip naked in an alley. He then proceeded to rape me. I was helpless and hopeless as he threatened me with his service revolver. He pointed a fully loaded 9 millimeter gun to my head, telling me to suck his penis. He threatened to kill me if I reported him. There was no doubt in my mind that he would've killed me if I did not obey his command. Today it's hard for me to even imagine that took place. However, back in that day, it was just a part of my crazy life. And because God had a calling on my life He didn't allow me to die, in either situation. In the midst of all my chaos and confusion, God rebuked death on my behalf, numerous times, because God had a greater purpose for me. He knew that buried underneath all my layers of filth, dirt, shame and disgust, I had a "Yes, Lord" for Him and one day it would come out. And when it came out I would dedicate my life to Him. My mother believed it too. Back then, only she and Jesus knew I would make it into the Kingdom of God. That's the reason she was able to stand throughout all my mess. Sometimes I cry when I think about all the awful things I did to her, yet she still loved me. She knew I was in a demonic struggle because the Word of God says: *"For we wrestle not against flesh and blood, but against principalities, against powers, against the rulers of the darkness of this world, against spiritual wickedness in high places."* That's why when she caught me stealing her money to go buy crack, she didn't run off in a corner and hide. It broke her heart but she didn't close the door on me or our relationship. Instead, she went into her secret closet, prayed and fasted for my deliverance. When some of her neighbors told her they saw me out tricking in Derby Park, it hurt and angered her, but she didn't put her head under a pillow and pretend it was not true or try to deny that I was demon possessed. She continued praying for the stronghold to be broken. A lot of parents know their children are involved in sin and unrighteousness but they are in denial and try to hide it from everyone, but not my mother. She wanted the prayers of the righteous because she believed the Word of God that said they availeth much. The one thing she never did was blame God for my condition or her pain. But instead she said like Job, *"Though He slay me yet will I trust Him."* Her faith and trust in her relationship with God answered her effectual, fervent prayers. My mother didn't have to be here to see my deliverance because she knew in whom she believed. She died knowing one day I would be free from addiction. That's what I call Blessed Assurance.

Since being saved and chosen by God, there have been a number of times in my life that I prayed for things and they didn't come to pass.

But that only forced me to pray harder. Besides, who hasn't asked God for things and He didn't grant them. Some people get disappointed, some get angry but I have grown enough in grace to know when things don't come to pass they are not in His perfect will. I know first-hand, people who prayed for sick loved ones, some even in my very own family, and they didn't get better, in fact they died. It hurts but everything God does is good and right even if causes us hurt and pain. We don't know the mind of God and His ways are past finding out. He moves how He sees fit. Just know that if you are a believer ALL things are working together for your good and the more you seek the Lord and listen to Him speak, things will be revealed to you. It took me a while to understand God's process, but the more I study and listen the more I learn.

Chapter Three

"Watch over your heart with all diligence,
for from it flow the springs of life."

G rowing up like most children I was influenced by my family, friends and neighborhood. Those three groups play a big part in helping shape who you become. Like many children who grow up in the inner city, I was bombarded with negative images, encounters and experiences. When drugs, crime and violence are all around you, whether you realize it or not, you are affected. Now when I take a real, open and honest look back at my life, through the lenses of salvation, I've come to the realization that I lived through some serious trauma. I'm not talking about some random events; I'm talking about several years of trauma. That's no exaggeration. My family life was chaotic and dysfunctional. I witnessed things in my home. Any psychologist or psychiatrist, and I have been to a whole lot of them, will tell you that what you experience in childhood affects you throughout life. When you experience the degree of trauma and abuse that I did, it affects you in many different ways. It can even change your destination and sometimes puts you on a path of devastation. The childhood trauma I endured led me on a path of destruction and I didn't have the ability to stop. I never dreamed that I would try drugs and immediately be hooked. Hooked to the point that I was completely powerless and possessed by demonic spirits.

Imagine being in such a horrible place of knowing what to do (which is stop using drugs) to get better but not having the ability to do it. It's not like I started out wanting to be a crackhead. No sane person starts out with the intention of ruining their lives. But in life, you never know where you will end up. A few poor decisions, and you can end up in a world of trouble. Who in the world would want to live such a life? When I was young, I had goals and dreams. My career goal was to become a nurse. My stepfather's sister, Madeline, was a registered nurse. I always looked up to her. She was an amazing woman who looked sharp and impressive in her white nurse's uniform. I remember my mother had a beautiful framed picture of her. I would look at the picture and say one day that will be me. I wanted to be just like her; she was a great role model.

Now, I wasn't the greatest student, but whenever I set my mind on something I get it accomplished. That's a good trait that comes from my OCD. But crack takes away everything. Trust me, I am a living witness. You can find yourself homeless and strung out. One day I was living the good life and one week later, I was strung out, working the streets, tricking. At the end of the day, I can't blame anyone for my actions, I am completely responsible. No one forced that crack pipe to my mouth.

Low self-esteem and a low sense of self-worth were motivating factors, but my desire to please the man who I thought was everything, my hero, proved to be the strongest force. That very man took my hand and led me into the ruthless, destructive and demonic underworld of addiction.

Chapter Four

I tell parents to be extremely careful with what they allow their kids to be exposed to in life. I tell them to protect children because they are your heart. The book of Proverbs says, *"Guard your heart above all else, for it determines the course of your life."* When kids are not protected and prepared for the world, they become easy prey.

As wild and crazy as my life turned out to be, I felt as though it started out pretty normal. Most of my early childhood memories before the age of eight are pretty enjoyable. Nothing really traumatic occurred during that time, as far as I can remember. But after all the mind-altering drugs I consumed for more than 30 years, I am amazed I can even remember that far back. Yet, I can and I clearly remember living in a loving and caring household. More specifically, I should say I remember feeling special and much loved by my mother. Although at times we had a two-parent family, it was my mother who really ran the show and kept our home together. However, even though she was queen of the house, she couldn't control everything that was happening; her plate was full. Managing me, my brothers and sisters, as well as trying to make a marriage work with a difficult man who had his own issues, was no easy task. As a result, there was a lot of instability and dysfunction surrounding me that she wasn't able to prevent.

Again, I didn't completely understand the level of dysfunction and trauma I endured until I started the process of writing this book. So many of my repressed memories have now been unlocked and uncovered. Things that I had buried deep inside of me came rising to the surface, forcing me to face them head on. I shed a few tears, reliving some of those hard memories. I even considered not sharing them. But I promised myself I would be completely transparent in this memoir. This means I have to be the real Bethann, raw and uncut. I must give the unedited version of my long road to redemption. So here I am, naked and completely open on the pages of this book. And if I can help someone who is suffering, especially with drug addiction, to face their demons, then it will all be worth it.

This has been an emotionally draining process. Memories are constantly popping into my head. Things that I had completely blocked out have made their way to the forefront of my mind. Things that I just dismissed as a child were actually far worse than I acknowledged back then. I came to the realization that a lot of stuff we experience and believe to be normal really isn't normal. We just accept it and deal with it, some of us better than others. But in fact, a lot of it is abnormal, toxic and emotionally crippling. However, somehow we find a way to cope with it. My family lived what most consider an average, lower-middle class lifestyle by today's standards. We didn't have a lot of money but nobody in the projects did. My mother's bank account wasn't bubbling over. We were probably a few paychecks away from homelessness and poverty. Even though my stepfather was working and hustling, things still came up short. I'm sure there were times my mother probably received extra help from the government. I had my share of grilled cheese sandwiches made from that great big block of cheese that didn't have a label and simply said cheese. But around my way, back then, everybody had those sandwiches and the macaroni and cheese from that big block. You can say it stuck to your ribs. We were glad to have it and didn't have time to be ashamed. Regardless, I recall very clearly seeing my mother work hard to make sure our family had everything we needed. I dedicated this book to my mother because she meant the world to me and petitioned the Lord for my deliverance. If it had not been for her prayers and the Lord on my side, upon my death, in hell is where I would have lifted up my eyes. Her determination and faithfulness, changed my destiny.

Whenever I talk about growing up, I always tell people that I know my mother did the best she could. She may have taken a few shortcuts in her life. But I never judged her for doing what she had to do to take care of her children. It's easy to sit back and judge someone until you have to walk a mile in their shoes. However, when you have children of your own, you are amazed at the lengths you will go to provide for them. I remember at one of my lowest points, when I was getting high, going into the stores in downtown Boston, boosting school clothes for my son so he would have nice things and the other kids wouldn't make fun of him. Even though I was strung out, I still wanted to try and be there for him in some kind of way. Therefore, anything my mother did to help provide for us, I know she did out of love. She was on her grind and I got nothing but respect for it.

During those early years of my life, we lived in the projects of Orchard Park (OP) in the Roxbury section of Boston. Orchard Park was one of the roughest, toughest and most dangerous areas in the city of Boston, and probably the country. You had to be aware of your surroundings. The neighborhood was overrun with guns, drugs, violence and prostitution. The police were even fearful around my neighborhood; so much so that they let a lot of things go. It was the last place you'd want to be caught on payday Friday. But it was normal to me. If you mention OP projects to anyone from Boston, the hair on their neck stands up. That place was like a war zone for many years. But my family managed to shield us from all the craziness that was going on within the development. Back then, it was like a great big family to me. There is an old African proverb that says "It takes a Village to raise a child." OP was that village. Families watched out for each other's children. Every kid had a bunch of aunties and uncles that were not related by blood. We called them that out of respect. They were able to discipline us when we got out of line and our parents were not around. They didn't really beat us, but they could smack us if we were really tripping. Nowadays, DSS and every child protective agency will be at your door if you even yell at a bad kid. But back then, the Village protected its own. We shared our resources so if our house ran out of sugar or flour or whatever, we could go down the hall to a neighbor's house and borrow what we needed. They could do the same in their time of need.

To me, it was a good place to live. With all the things my mother was trying to balance, I'm amazed she had time for anything else. But I remember her cleaning all the time. Cleaning might have been

36

therapeutic for her or maybe just one of things she had full control over. Either way, she kept our apartment immaculate. My mother made sure our house was neat and always clean. You could eat off the floor. We didn't need the five-second rule because every spot of our house was flawless. My mother had that old time belief that cleanliness was next to Godliness. She took pride in our home and devoted special attention to detail. In fact I can remember one year we won first place for the best decorated apartment in the projects.

Holidays were also super important to her. My mother made sure we had great celebrations. Christmas was really special. She would go over the top for Christmas. Let me tell you, there is nothing she wouldn't do to make sure we had the best Christmas possible. Every year we got all kinds of toys and clothes. All that stuff had to cost a lot of money. In hindsight, I'm sure some of our gifts probably came from Globe Santa and other charities. But to a kid who just wants to wake up Christmas morning to a few presents under the tree, it meant a lot. I only have one child and can't imagine trying to make it happen with five or six kids in the house. But we never missed a beat. Shortly after my sixth birthday, the Lord moved us out of OP. I say the Lord because it was He, Jehovah Jireh (Lord that Provides) who helped my mother by making provisions for us to move. The projects served a purpose and was a decent place to live, but they were really not designed to live in for a lifetime. Anyways, it was a safe place for us for the time we lived there because we had no idea how dangerous and deadly Orchard Park really was. I had some good times in that place, but there were also some not-so-good things that happened while I lived there. As I previously said, my mother did the best she could but the reality is that sometimes your best isn't good enough. I'm not being critical or completely blaming my mother for the negative things that happened to me and the underlying dysfunction that hovered over us like a black cloud. But if I'm going to be completely honest and maintain integrity in my word, she does bear some responsibility for not keenly watching and ensuring my safety. Although the molestation started inside the four walls of that apartment on 2 Bean Ct. in Orchard Park, it continued on 25 Hammond Street, the place we moved to next and stayed throughout my childhood. The molestation was not only in our home, but in the homes of several families.

Again, if I'm being completely honest, it occurred at times where she put me in harm's way, albeit unintentional, it's a fact. In no way do I blame her for the actions of others, but I believe had she made some better and different choices, things might have been a little different. My life may have taken a different path.

Chapter Five

*"Behold, children are a heritage from
the Lord fruit of the womb a reward."
Psalm 127:3."*

I can't say enough about all the great things my
mother did for me. In spite of the fact that I might
be critical of a few decisions she made, the last
thing I want anyone to think is that my mother didn't
do everything she could to take the best care of me.
When I got hooked on drugs, it devastated her. She
tried to move heaven and earth to get me saved, clean
and sober. She knew that once the Lord saved me,
then other things would happen. She prayed and
fasted. She laid down in sack cloth and ashes on
church altars all across Massachusetts and in her own

prayer closet. Her prayers and dedication to my deliverance are the main reasons I'm saved and serving the Lord today and not still strung out chasing cars down Blue Hill Ave. for my next "Hit" of crack. I'll keep saying it over and over; she never gave up on me or the promise that God made her concerning me. In all of her amazement and commitment to me she still had her flaws. Inadvertently, she passed some of them down to me. Please don't let anyone ever try and convince you that generational curses don't exist. I'm a living witness that they do. Some of my mother's personal demons were transferred to me. Some people don't believe that demons are real. They think the spiritual realm is made up; but as a child, I knew spirits existed. I'd seen them in people and cast out of people. They are real. And trust me, if one gets ahold of you, I guarantee you will be willing to do anything to get free.

Some of my mother's other personal characteristics were passed down to me as well. One of the concerns with writing the book is that people can take out of context the things I share about my family. The problem with being open and honest about your life is it doesn't always paint your family in the best light. When you are completely honest, sometimes there are unintended consequences and collateral damage. Every family has secrets with things they don't want made public, let alone displayed all over the pages of a book. Family secrets are not always bad, but they are secrets for a reason. Therefore, I don't want my truth to hurt or tarnish the legacy of any of my loved ones, especially my mother. Nor do I want to damage the credibility of my living relatives because of past indiscretions and poor choices. There is an old saying that says you should "Let sleeping dogs lie." So that put me in a dilemma as I struggled with what to include in this book.

Do I tell the most unadulterated, unfiltered, honest version of my testimony and let the chips fall where they may or do I exclude key elements and dress up dirty truths to spare the feeling of the ones I love? The truth is there was so much dysfunction in my life that I could fill the pages of several novels. But where dysfunction abounds in my life, love was more abundant. The Bible lets us know that love covers a multitude of sins. And where molestation and physical abuse were present, grace and mercy helped me make it through my toughest times. However, it wasn't easy and it wasn't normal and it wasn't anything a kid should ever have to endure.

Molestation is a sneaky, secret form of sexual abuse that was rampant in my childhood. The slick predators were very manipulative and subtle with their ways. They are incredible deceivers, which is why my molestation was able to continue from age six until my young adulthood. Several men and women, who were supposed to be safe people in my life, inappropriately touched and fondled me. While they didn't go as far as to rape me, and I'm grateful, they did violate and damage me. These people were slimy. They presented their abuse in an innocent way. They convinced us that it was sex play and not real. We thought we were playing house and doctor. That's the way they justified the inappropriate touches. They were really sick people who used us to fulfill their sexual perversions. They got off watching us lay in the bed touching and rubbing on each other. Some went further and got in the bed and got on top of me, while rubbing my genitals. This happened so many times throughout my childhood with different family members and friends of family. The worst thing about it is that it happened so much until I thought it was normal. And as sick as it sounds, I started to like it. There was one adult male I loved to visit. He made me feel like a princess. I would get excited and dress up when I was going to his house because I knew what was going to happen. I liked it so much that the victim cycle came full circle and I went from being a victim to a perpetrator. I started doing it to others in my house.

I told you I was going to be all the way real with my testimony. The molestation turned me into a sex fiend who was willing to do anything sexually. All of this happened right under my mother's nose. My mother did the best she could do. I don't really blame her because she was not in her right state of mind because that thorazine had her shuffling all around the apartment.

Chapter Six

*"The scales begin to fall off my eyes and
I start to see things as they really are."*

Around the time I turned eight is when I believe my eyes started opening up to the reality of my surroundings and more importantly to the dysfunction of my family life. As a young child, the Lord gave me vision to see things in the spiritual and natural realm. However, some things I saw as a kid, I didn't always understand. I began to notice that things were not as pleasant as I once thought they were in my home.

One of the first things that I began to take notice of was that my father was away from the house more and more frequently. He would go missing and there'd be no discussion about it. That, in itself, wasn't necessarily strange because he and mother had created this fantasy that he was a world famous actor. As kids, we are naïve and tend to believe anything our parents tell us. So when he was gone away for long periods of time and they said he was off in Hollywood acting in a movie, we believed it. It's amazing the level of deceitfulness parents will stoop to try and keep things away from their children. I know it wasn't done maliciously but rather just to keep us away from the drama of his life. They had us convinced he was superman, the real life, white, Clark Kent, Superman. That's what they said and that's what we believed.

We believed that when he wasn't around, he was in Hollywood, where they would apply makeup to turn him into Superman. We would gather around the television and watch daddy, as he saved the day. He was a larger than life superhero to us. He was tall and handsome and fit the part of a Hollywood leading man. And when he wasn't out of town acting in movies, he was a small business owner along with some other side hustles. One of his side businesses was a bait and tackle store where the local fisherman would go and buy products.

What we didn't know was that his real job was a pimp. His pimping had a devastating effect on my mother which turned my household upside down. His hatred of monogamy chipped away at my mother's self-worth and sanity. He nearly drove her crazy. The streets have a saying that you can't turn a Ho into a housewife. But I have a saying that you can't turn a pimp into a loving and responsible husband. It's not in his nature. As they say "It is what it is." I think my siblings, who were extremely resilient, just carried on and were less affected than me and my mother. My mother acted out in several ways. She did some creeping herself. It probably made her feel better in the moment, but it didn't diminish her pain or give her any real satisfaction. His actions sent her into a deep depression causing her to behave strangely and display signs of instability. Slowly, but steadily, she morphed into a different person. She became a shell of herself. She was a sad, angry woman coming to the realization that she no longer, if she ever really was, her husband's priority. Faced with the realty of her situation, my mother had become more withdrawn and started experiencing severe mood swings. She would isolate herself in her bedroom and sometimes go into fits of rage and break and destroy things. This bizarre behavior led to her leaving the home for days at a time. We later found out that she had been placed in a psychiatric hospital to stabilize her.

Later in life, she would joke about her jaunts at the "crazy house." In no way am I making light of mental illness. Mental illness is real and it affects families more than we know. I'm just recalling conversations with my mom. Her long bouts with mental illness, along with my father's issues caused our home to become fractured, and dysfunction became the norm. The dysfunction led to severe changes in our family. While mother was in treatment, different family members would stay with us. And sadly, the molestation and sexual abuse continued for years, by both male and female perpetrators.

Chapter Seven

"Demand excellence from your children and they will rise to the occasion. Without expectations, they will be lost."

Around the age of 14, things began to get a little more stable in my family. I was still dealing with molestation issues and had a lot of different emotions going on inside of me. When I turned 13, mother gave her life to the Lord and joined a church. She jumped full fledge into the ministry. She was completely consumed. The church she joined was a staunch, Pentecostal ministry that had some strict practices. Some of them were really extreme and outdated but since we were part of the ministry we followed them. For example, they didn't allow woman to wear pants. They believed pants were for men only. They took the literal meaning from the Book of Deuteronomy 22:5: *"The woman shall not wear that which pertaineth unto a man, neither shall a man put on a woman's garment: for all that do so are abomination unto the Lord thy God."* We couldn't even wear makeup and some women, the older ones, covered their heads in the sanctuary. They believe the structure enabled people to live holy. Although it seemed to be a bit much, we did witness miracles, signs and wonders. In that house of God there was true deliverance. We had numerous services throughout the week, like evangelism and Bible study. We would also have routine street meetings and shuts-ins, where we were closed in the church for days at a time, fasting and praying, seeking a closer relationship with the Lord. My mother's world revolved around the church and everything else took a back seat, even her children.

God has an order for His people and the family is important. You really can't serve God in the capacity that you have been called to if your natural house is not in order. An important thing for people to learn is that a personal relationship with the Lord is not regimented or owned by any one religion or denomination. When you give your life to the Lord you create a personal relationship with Him. Far too many preachers and churches have caused people to turn away from God because they perverted His word. They placed requirements and restrictions on the people of God that are not biblical or even scripturally based in truth.

Unfortunately, the church we joined had some practices that were not Kingdom requirements but rather church doctrine. And, even as a teenager who had experienced a lot trauma, I knew all that was preached was not of God.

Chapter Eight

*"He who finds a wife finds what is
good and obtains favor from the Lord."*
Proverbs 18:22

B e extremely cautious when you are deciding on someone with whom you plan to share your life. Choosing the wrong person could lead you to a life of heartache and misery. On many occasions, people have allowed good looks and lust of the heart to lead them to terrible places, including death. The last thing anyone wants is a fatal attraction. So, it behooves you to be prayerful and guard your heart. King Solomon, the wisest man to ever live, admonished us in the Book of Proverbs 4:23:

"Guard your heart above all else, for it determines the course of your life." Notwithstanding, I believe the heart, just like everything else in our lives, must come under subjection and be managed. The famous poet, Emily Dickinson, said "The heart wants what it wants." She is right. However, a lot of times it's not the heart that wants but rather the flesh that wants. Either way, I caution you not to fall victim to that claim but rather take heed to the Prophet Jeremiah who said: *"The heart is deceitful above all things, and desperately wicked: who can know it?"* Clearly the heart is critical not only to our natural being but also to our spiritual being.

We should commit ourselves to never make decisions or take actions based on feelings of the heart that can change at any given time. Furthermore, this may sound old fashioned to some but we, as women, should not be picking our mates. Yes, that's right. We should not be picking our mates. In 2019 I'm sure that sounds archaic and crazy to a lot of people. We have a strong feminist movement and the world is changing. Women run major companies, countries and sit in high political offices. While all that is well and true I take my position from the Word of God. In the Book of Proverbs, which is full of nuggets of wisdom, the writer lets us know that: *"He who finds a wife finds a good thing and obtains favor from the Lord."* Therefore, I believe it's not mine or any woman's place to go looking for a husband. Thus no matter what movements occur in society and the world, I stand on the Book of Malachi 3:6, *"I am the Lord I change not."* When we go contrary to God's order, we tread on dangerous grounds. Trust me, this is one instruction we should definitely take literally. I've been married twice. Both of my marriages failed miserably and the first one nearly cost me my life. Neither marriage was sanctioned by God because I chose the men. As a result, I suffered and lived a hard life. But I have repented to God.

So please, I implore you to wait patiently on God to send you a mate. Sadly, I got caught chasing the man I thought was my hero. In the end, he turned out to be nothing more than a zero. For a while, I was in denial of who he was. But if you wait long enough, a leopard will show his spots. There's an old saying— "Love will make you do stupid things." I did a lot of stupid things trying to keep the man I thought was

Mr. Right and they all came to naught. Women, I believe in God's time he will send you your own Boaz or knight in shining amour or at the least the right man, who will love, honor and protect you. He may not be that tall, dark and handsome man you dreamed of or should I say lusted after. However, if he is sent by God, you will be blessed and your life will be fulfilled; that is as long as you do your part by holding up your responsibility to your mate.

And men, consult God when choosing a wife. Seek a woman that you can love, honor, provide for and protect. Find a woman that stimulates you in every way. Don't get caught up in looks only. I know it's easy and feels good for the moment, but that moment doesn't last long. Beauty fades. Sometimes what we think is beauty is just a façade. Women are going to the Dominican Republic and different places getting all kinds of breast and butt implants. Men and women are tricking other people into believing they are something they are not. Take the advice of a few young men, Michael, Rickey and Ronnie, who grew up around my housing project and formed the hip-hop group, BBD (Bell, Biv, Devoe). They said "You can't trust a big butt and smile." It pains me to say in a lot of cases they were right. I saw a lot of men in the street fall prey to a big butt and a smile. I fell for a handsome guy in a suit, working behind the counter of my father's Bait and Tackle shop.

That store played a crucial role in my life. It's the place where I first saw Black, my future husband. My stepfather's business partner Slim, who I had a crush on. I snuck down there one day trying to see if he was around. He was way too old for me but I wanted to see if I flirted with him would he respond. I wasn't thinking about having sex with him but I would have allowed him to touch and grind on me. The molestation had me really messed up and made me hypersexual.

Slim wasn't there. Instead, there stood Black at the counter and he was looking fly. He was working with my brothers so I didn't dare go in because I wasn't even supposed to be down there. But I was definitely going to find out more about Black. When my brothers got home I asked one of my brothers for his number. I called him that night and we started talking, every day. My life would never be the same. We would have a child, get married and go on the wildest, craziest adventure that led me into a life of addiction.

Our flesh will always seek to gratify itself and nothing good comes from it. Discipline and order have to be in every area of our lives, especially our relationships and marriages.

Chapter Nine

*"Be careful who you let speak
over and into your life."*

To say that my marriage to Black was destiny might be a stretch, but there were forces in our families that were really trying hard to push us down the wedding aisle. My mother was one of the main people who wanted me to marry him. I think she was compelled from a biblical standpoint. It had to be because she and Black's mother were not the best of friends. In the past, she and Black's mother competed for the affection of the same man, my stepfather. I got caught up in the middle of their games at times. As I said previously, my stepfather was a pimp who had several women, and Black's mother was one of his special ladies. Why my mother would want me to have anything to do with that family was beyond me. But my mother was truly saved and rose above the nonsense. She believed marriage was the best thing for me. It made sense as Black and I had history. We started going together when I was 16. It wasn't love at first site, but it was close. I wanted to be with him from the moment I walked into my stepfather's store and saw him behind the counter. We connected immediately and started hanging tough. Not long after, we had a child together. Black had gone to Chicago. When he returned, Black decided we should live together. Because we were shacking and living in sin, my mother wanted us to marry. During that time she was heavy into the church. The Lord was moving in her life and she was deepening her relationship with God. Her focus was on the scripture, "It's better to marry than to burn." She didn't want her daughter going to hell.

Although I loved Black and wanted to marry him, he had a dark side that was all too familiar. He was a little too cool and a little too slick, or so he thought. But I had seen his style before; it wasn't original. I grew up with pimps all around me, even though it took me until my later teenage years to get a real understanding of that world. However, when the blinders were taken off, I understood everything that had been hiding in plain sight before me. I also understood why my mother shielded me from all that came with that life. But everything about Black screamed that life. Black reminded me so much of my stepfather in a lot of ways. Little did I know, he was more like him than I even imagined. That was not a good thing at all. All the red flags and warning signs didn't matter. I believed Black was trying to be the man I wanted. He was discreet with his dirt. He was playing his position all the way. Black was going to church with me regularly. He even professed that he had given his life to the Lord and was saved. He was taking Bible classes and learning the Word of God.

Every Saturday my mother would hold prayer service at her house. There would be a lot of saints who came over to fellowship. I wanted all of them to get to know the man that was in my life. So, I started working on Black to get him to come to the prayer service. Finally, I convinced him to come. During the prayer, my aunt, who is actually my mother's cousin, began to prophesy to me and Black. She said while in the spirit she saw a brass ring around us. There was the confirmation I needed. I think that was also the moment my mother started planning our wedding. When someone you knew who was saved told you they got a Word from God, you believed it. You didn't challenge them because they were more seasoned than you. I love my aunt and I'm sure she meant well but that could never work on me now. Again, it goes back to my mother saying "You have to know the Lord for yourself."

A lot of people look for prophesy and like to get a good word about their finances or blessings coming, but keep in mind true prophesy doesn't always give good reports. The prophets of old spoke of doom, gloom and destruction. But today everybody is next in line for a blessing. Some people are willing to stand in line and wait their turn for a good word. But all prophesy is not real. And there is an abundance of false prophesies. It's not always done to hurt you. But it's manipulative and born of flesh. False prophesy can lead you into a fire. So, anytime someone offers you a word of prophesy don't just accept it. It's your responsibility to try that spirit by the Word of God. But truth be told, I didn't really need her prophesy, convincing or encouraging me when it came to Black. I thought that man was my hero. I wanted to be married to him. No one needed to push me, encourage me or *proph-a-lie* to me. For years, I had dreamed of the day we would live the fairy tale life. I just knew one day he would take me away and we would live happily ever after. He was my knight in shining amour. But those dreams were actually delusions. Delusions that I convinced myself would one day come to pass, but instead turned into nightmares. When I woke up out of that fantasy, I knew that happily-ever-after wasn't going to be the case. Still, given everything I knew, I was down to try and make the best of things. I was going to take those lemons and turn them into lemonade. I was going to take that wannabe, hustling pimp, who I loved with all my heart, and ride with him until the wheels fell off. And naively believed I could turn him into the man I wanted to be. I was the Bonnie to his Clyde, and I was down for whatever, whenever as long as it meant being with him. I loved this man with every fiber of my being. Not to be corny, but I felt he completed me. The sad part was that he didn't love me the way I loved him.

There were some clear signs that maybe I was in for more than I bargained. One of the signs hit me right across my head one night. That sign was his closed fist. Any man that loves you wouldn't beat you. I say that now after having been redeemed. But I had lived through so much dysfunction and saw my mother get beat so many times that I thought his actions were normal. But his first time should have been his last time. Things could only get worse. Maya Angelou said "When someone shows you who they are believe them; the first time." Not me, I still believed we could make it work. I should have listened to that old saying "Denial is not a river in Egypt" because my denial was on a 100. Still I kept pressing on, digging a deeper hole into a world of abuse, deceit and dysfunction that was so comfortable and familiar to me. But hey things can change—can't they?

Chapter Ten

"Why did I say I do?"

After all the mess I had been through with Black, you would think I would have just cut my losses and moved on. But no, I still wanted to be his wife and he wanted to be my husband just as bad. We were two dysfunctional peas in a pod. My embarrassing need for a hero in my life, along with my self-esteem issues, pushed me into his arms. Ego, lust and Black's desire to be "the man" was his motivation to keep me by his side. I was the trophy he loved to display on his arms. Young and very attractive, I stood six feet tall with a banging body. I don't say any of that out of conceit, those were his words. That was just the way it was. I was a dime piece, he knew it. He loved the way I looked and made him feel. He loved the fact that I was his and would parade me around in front of his boys like I was his prized possession. He would dress me up and get my hair braided pretty. Plenty of dudes would try to "holla" at me whenever we were out together. They were thirsty and would tell him, "You better not mess up with her or we will be right there to take her off your hands." He knew they were serious and he wasn't going to give them the opportunity.

Both of us just accepted the inevitable that marriage was in the cards. The only problem was we were not moving fast enough for my mother. So she decided to take things into her own hands. I know she meant well, however, it was my life and my decision to make. But that never stopped her before, why would this time be any different. My mother and I had an interesting relationship. She taught me everything I know, the good as well as the not so good. She was a mastermind at getting her way and sometimes that meant doing things that some might consider questionable. Now, please don't misconstrue what I am saying. By no means was she evil or a vicious person at all. She was resourceful, filled with love and willing to do whatever was necessary to achieve her goals. Somebody said "Use what you got to get what you want." I get a lot of my determination from her. It's a personality trait that she handed down to me. With her infectious smile, my mother could light up a room, and with her clever wit she was able to pull all kinds of strings. I watched and I emulated her. We had heart-to-hearts and fireside mother-daughter chats. She taught me the real game of life. She taught me all about men and how I should carry myself with them. She taught me how to massage and stroke a man's ego to get him to do whatever you wanted. She taught me the way to a man's heart was through his stomach and she taught me how to keep them satisfied. And satisfying them had very little to do with sex, but she taught me about that too. That's something missing today, mothers teaching daughters.

My mother was something else and she had it going on. And like I said, she wanted me married. She was tired of waiting for us to get it together. We had accepted the Lord and were living saved. We had our son with us and were planning to have another child. We had some order in our lives. Plus, we had received the prophetic word about marriage from my mother's cousin. So what were we waiting for? We went ahead and set a date. We didn't make a big announcement. My mother was the only one who knew about our plans.

We talked to our Pastor and told him about our intentions to marry. We asked him if he would marry us. He agreed to do the ceremony but not until we completed three counseling sessions with him. Nowadays, I think they call it pre-marital counseling. They do it to make sure that both the man and woman are ready to make that life-long commitment. After completing the counseling sessions, we were set to get married. The wedding was going to be at our apartment at 10 Hammond Street. I went out and bought a nice outfit. Black wore blue jeans and a basic shirt. Even though it was at our apartment, I still wanted to look nice. I was dressed up and he was dressed down. We were already starting on the wrong foot. The Bible says, *"How can two walk together except they agree."* Nevertheless, we went ahead with the ceremony. We said our "I do's" and that was that. It wasn't anything like you dream of as a little girl. I dreamed my wedding day would be big, but that's life. It was a little disappointing but it wasn't the end of the world.

The marriage started out pretty good. Our union was official in the eyes of society, and we were respecting God's order. Black seemed to be trying. A lot of the drama and abuse had stopped. I kind of felt the worst of times was behind us. Maybe Black was a changed man and we could live a normal life. Me, Black, and our son were a real family. Every day seemed to be a little better. Black and I were together day and night. It was good to me because I could keep a close eye on him and his wandering eye. I got him a job with me at Blue Cross Blue Shield Insurance Company. It was a good job at the time. We worked with a lot of cool people. He was a little too friendly with some of the girls but he wasn't disrespectful. Of course later on I found out he had been creeping with a few of them. When we were not working, we were at church. We were living a saved life, well at least I was. Black was acting the part of the saved father and head of the house for a while. Every once in a while we would take weekend trips to different places. Black's uncle and his girlfriend were our hanging partners. We would travel a lot to Cape Cod and Maine. Black loved to go to Maine because he knew his way around the state. We would stay at some nice places. Of course later on I found out he used to pimp women up in Maine. But during the time I was completely clueless and it was always a nice getaway.

Those were some fun times in my marriage. We would go away but never did anything that was crazy. They would drink a little beer and alcohol. I was committed to living a saved life. Black knew right from wrong. He was a grown man and had to make his own choices. They say you don't backslide overnight. They say it's a gradual process. I saw that process happening right before my eyes. His drinking became more frequent. Then things advanced. The men started going off from us to smoke weed. I never saw them do it, but I knew what it smelled like. So when they came back, reeking of marijuana, I figured they must of smoked some. And for a while, it didn't get any worse than that. I didn't want him to smoke but it wasn't the end of the world, and I sort of believed he would stop at some point.

We were both supposed to be living saved, but Black had his own version of salvation. It wasn't the version I studied and learned about from the Bible. He was trying to keep it together until I started to notice some odd behavior. Whenever we were hanging out and having a good time, Black would sneak off with his uncle or by himself for a little while. I would look up and he would be gone. I would say, "Where the heck did he go?" Then he would come back looking different, but he didn't have a weed smell on him. I would question him and ask why he disappeared and what was he doing. He assured me it was nothing, but I knew better. I was not naïve about men playing games because I had seen it my whole life. I just wanted to know what kind of game he was playing. I was hoping he wasn't out messing around with another woman. I continued to watch him and his suspicious behavior increased. Then Black started going out to bars and parties without me. I was hurt. All I wanted to do was be with my husband and now he was excluding me from things and I didn't understand. I urge all women and men to watch the behavior of your spouses and significant others. Anytime people are doing things uncharacteristic of their behavior, there is a reason. I promise you there is something going on. They used to call it a woman's intuition. I'm not quite sure what they call it for men, but having given my life to the Lord, in the spirit realm, we call it discernment; and one thing I think all believers should pray for is keen discernment. Having that gift will prevent you from entering a lot of bad situations.

Anyways, Black's behavior and attitude got worse. He started to change. One night I worked up the courage to confront him. I sat him down and pleaded with him to tell me what was going on and why was he was excluding me from parts of his life. I blamed myself. What could I do to make things better? I asked Black to tell me what had changed in our relationship so I could fix it. We went back and forth over a few conversations. He didn't want to tell me. I just knew it was another woman. Finally, one day, when he couldn't take my pestering any longer, he broke down and told me the truth. He said, "Listen I have not been messing around with anybody else, but I have been doing a little more than the alcohol and marijuana. I have been using cocaine. I started smoking it and now I can't stop." "What? Why? That's what you have chosen over me? That's what you have been neglecting me for? Is it that good? If it means that much to you let me do it with you."

Chapter Eleven

"Cocaine is a hell of a drug."
Rick James

In the 1980's, President Ronald Regan initiated the "Say no to Drugs" campaign. It was a big deal because illegal drugs were ruining families and communities. People were getting high all over the country. Cocaine was big at that time. The Mexican cartels and some foreign governments had flooded the streets of America with it. It used to be the drug of choice for the rich and famous. You had to have money to enjoy it. But they changed the game, made it affordable so more people had access to it, including my husband, Black. God only knows how long Black had been using cocaine. Black had a habit and it was way worse than I realized at the time. He was hooked and I had no idea. Talk about naïve. Imagine living with someone, never knowing they were a full blown addict. You have to be really sick and slick to keep a secret like that from your wife. But here we go again with the secrets in my life. It seems like my life is full of people keeping secrets and shielding me from things. First it was mother and family, now it's my husband. Why do all the people I love keep secrets, especially the ones that affect my life?

I really don't know how long Black had been using cocaine and spending all of our money. Back then the million dollar question for me was why would he choose that stuff over his family? Why did he feel the need to use all of our money on that mess? It didn't take long for me to get my answers. The drugs had taken over his life. He was powerless, just like every other addict. The first night when things came to a head and he let me know about his cocaine use, he brought me into our living room. He pulled out two vials filled with white powder and placed them on the table. Then he said, "This is what I have been doing. It's cocaine." He said "I don't want you involved because this is bad news." I was a little shocked but it really didn't seem like a big deal to me. I was more relieved that it wasn't another woman he had been messing around with or chasing. But he really was chasing that "white girl" and I'm not talking about a Caucasian woman. That's a street term we use for cocaine. I got high for so long I know them all. Anyways, that night I said "Let me try it." Black agreed. He showed me what to do. I put some on my tongue and on the top of my gums. I had what they call a freeze. I wasn't impressed at all. I said to myself, this is what he is choosing over spending time with me. But since he liked it so much, I pretended to enjoy it too. However, sniffing it really didn't have any effect on me. My desire for it never increased, I was still trying to live saved. Truly the only real thing it did in my eyes was waste our money. Black was still behaving very secretively. My intuition wouldn't rest, there was still something not quite right about the whole situation. Black wasn't as slick as he thought. It was clear that he was still hiding something from me and I knew it. He was still sneaking off and excluding me from things. I knew about the cocaine, we were doing it together. There was no need for him to sneak away, that is unless there was something else that he was trying to keep away from me. I confronted him again and he was angry. I really didn't care because I was angry too. I needed to know the real deal. I was 100% loyal to him, and I wanted the same so I wasn't going to let this thing go until I was completely satisfied. I was convinced that there was no way some white powder could replace me in my husband's life. But I was wrong, it did. There was no doubt he enjoyed it more than me. I couldn't be in denial anymore. At that very moment, it was crystal clear that we were unequally yoked and my marriage was in real trouble. The Bible lets you know that when you are unequally yoked, the stronger will pull the weaker. And that's exactly what happened, because I wasn't willing to let anything or anybody replace me in Black's life. This man was my world and I still wasn't ready to let him go. And, if it meant indulging into whatever it took to keep him home at night, I was willing to do it. So I kept pestering him about what he was hiding from me. I wouldn't let it go. This went on for about a year. Black must have known I was beginning to figure things out. One Friday night when we both returned home from work, Black dropped our son off at his sister's house. He went out to run some errands, came back home and set up a romantic interlude. He had that look in his eyes. He was dancing sexy, trying to turn me on and rubbing up against me. I thought we were going to make love but that wasn't his plan. I now realize that was his happy place, just before he was about to get high. So the lights were dimmed and he put on some "feel-good music." I'll never forget the song he had playing on the stereo, it was, "Love Has Finally Come At Last" by Pattie Labelle and Bobby Womack. I can still hear that song playing in my ears today, as clear as it was that night, almost 40 years ago. I really thought we were going to have an intimate night together. That was our lovemaking music. But we were not making love that night, well at least not with each other. He had been in the kitchen cooking up something. He brought over a glass plate. On the plate were whitish, beige rocks and a small glass pipe. I wasn't sure what was really about to go down, but I just went with the flow since he was finally allowing me into this part of his life. Black said, "You know that cocaine that we been sniffing? Well this is the new way to use it. We take the powder and mix it with ammonia and it rocks up like these ones right here. Then you smoke it and its gets you 10 times higher than just sniffing it. It's called free-basing and it's no joke. You don't want to mess with this. It's on a whole different level." But it looked harmless to me. I said to him, "Is this really what you have been hiding from me? This is why you have been sneaking out and being suspicious? This is what you chose over me? It must really be the bomb." He said "Baby, it's out of this world." He then picked up the pipe and took two of the little rocks and put them into it. If you have ever been around a fiend, their whole demeanor changes before they get ready for that first hit. They go to another place. People used to use the old Star Trek term of beaming up to Scotty. He was on his way to that place of ecstasy as he prepared his blast. Black took his lighter and lit the pipe and took one hit. His eyes opened wide. He took another hit and he looked as if he was flying. It was a sight to see. Now it was my turn. Why didn't I just say never mind I'm all set? Why didn't I just leave the room and let him do his thing alone? Why? Why? Why? I had time to change my mind. But I was all in for my hero.

He loaded the pipe up again and passed it to me. He put it up to my mouth and he lit it. He instructed me to strongly inhale. He said "suck it harder." The first hit didn't do anything. Stupid me should have just stopped then. But no, I let him load up the pipe again. He told me to take another hit. Then I took another hit that was even bigger. Finally after about three or four hits, I felt it. That hit rocked my world and took me to a place I had never been before. A place I never wanted to leave. That feeling wore off quickly. I was ready for more. We smoked all the rocks he had. My husband went out and got some more and we smoked that whole night. I don't think I got an hour of sleep.

No matter how much I smoked I couldn't get that feeling back that I had from that first high. It didn't matter I was hooked that quickly. I would spend the next 30-something years trying to experience that feeling just one more time. It didn't happen. I fell into the trap that all fiends fall into chasing the impossible.

Chapter Twelve

*"The man I thought was a
Hero was actually a Zero."*

Remember earlier when I talked about prophesy? I told you that every prophesy you receive is not always authentic. An example is the day my mother's cousin prophesied that she saw a brass ring around me and Black. We should have waited for true confirmation before we got married because I know God didn't send Black to me. Black was sent from the pits of hell to abort the mission Christ had for my life. Before the foundation of the world was set, my mission was to help with the lost and help the hopeless find hope in God. The Bible says we wrestle not against flesh and blood but against powers and principalities and spiritual wickedness in high places. So I won't blame my mother's cousin for my marrying Black. I knew what he was. He was a violent, mean man. How I ever convinced myself that he was my hero is beyond me. He was nothing more than a coward. In fact, Black was a wolf in sheep's clothing. He was the seed of Judas. His betrayal to me and our marriage was epic. The Lord spared my life in spite of all of Black's attempts to destroy me. The treachery in the way he treated me was cunning. The way he pretended to protect me from crack was an Oscar worthy performance. Black knew once I got hooked on that freebase my life was over. No man that truly loved his wife would have done the things Black did to me. He should have stayed and finished Bible school and he would have heard the fifth Book of Ephesians that says: *"Husbands, love your wives, just as Christ also loved the church and gave Himself up for her."* But he was too busy trying to be a player. He grew up as a wannabe pimp, idolizing the game. So loving me as Christ loved the church was impossible for him. After a few years of marriage I completely gave up on the thought that he could ever be the hero I envisioned. The sad thing was that as bad as Black was as a husband, he was worse as a father. I knew and agreed to what I got myself into but my son was an innocent child. Black didn't even treat him good. Neither of us were perfect parents, but I never abused or purposely hurt our son. I'm a strong believer in discipline, my mother disciplined us. The Word of God is crystal clear about discipline: *"Those who spare the rod of discipline hate their children. Those who love their children care enough to discipline them."* Every child needs discipline and correction. But I draw the line, and so does the criminal justice system, when it comes to abuse. Some of the things Black did to our son were violently abusive, and he would have probably been prosecuted if he did them today. Once, he savagely beat our son with an extension cord. The beating was so severe that it caused some of his skin to fall off. Only a heartless animal could do that to his own flesh and blood. At the time our son was only five years old and basically still a baby. Black justified his actions by saying his grandmother used an extension cord on him when he was child and got out of line. I don't quite remember what my son did to provoke him to such rage, but nothing warranted the abuse.

Whatever the reason, to me it was a weak, lame excuse of a serial abuser. Like I said, I wasn't opposed to a spanking but what he did was so severe that our son needed medical attention. We brought our son to the hospital emergency room. The medical staff was horrified. I was completely honest with the doctors. I told them Black was responsible for our son's condition. I even told them he used an extension cord. They immediately notified the Department of Social Services. Now the government was involved with our family. We had to meet with a social worker who later came to our home and interviewed us both. In addition, we were required to take classes on parenting. We didn't need to take classes on parenting I wasn't the abuser, he was. However, we did everything DSS required and after some time they closed our case. To this day, that beating still haunts me. The look of helplessness that my son displayed is as vivid today as it was that morning. His desperate screams as he looked at me for protection still rings in my ears. It still brings tears to my eyes that I was unable to protect him from his enraged father, who was supposed to love and protect him. I wasn't aware of how sick Black really was. Back in the day when you did the kind of stuff he did, they would just call you "crazy." I'm sure now that he had some undiagnosed, mental health issues. That has to be the only explanation for the things he did. Black was so bad he even abused our dog and that is definitely a telltale sign of a disturbed individual.

I couldn't believe the day it happened. It was early in our marriage and we were both still working. One day after work we arrived home and the puppy had made a big mess around the house. It was pretty bad. There were paper towels and tissues all over the place. However, it wasn't like the house was destroyed. We were partly responsible for leaving the dog alone all day, as it was just a puppy. But Black was so enraged that he took it to the extreme. He went into our bedroom, grabbed a pair of gloves and beat the heck out of our poor, helpless puppy. Granted he made a mess and needed to be properly trained, but the way he beat that dog was not only uncalled for, but also sadistic. I should have taken my son and the puppy and got as far away from him as I could. But I was dumb and in love and wanted to be the best wife I could be and I put my husband before everything. I was following God's order, but Black wasn't. His abuse continued and caused me to change my whole life. My personality went from an extrovert to an introvert. I once was outgoing and a very social person and all that changed.

We began to fight all the time and I just allowed it to happen. All throughout my marriage I succumbed to his ways. I strongly believe that I was willing to endure Black's torment because I witnessed my mother take so much from her husband. Children model what they see their parents do and grow into them, whether negative or positive. I watched my mother accept things that I knew even as a child were not healthy for her mind or spirit. But it became normal to me. Dysfunction is a powerful thing. It normalizes abuse and neglect. It can make things seem wrong and other things seem right. I watched her do things just to please a man. And here I go, repeating the cycle. Here I go, so desperate to make my relationship work and hold on to a man that turned me out to drugs and abused us. If that isn't dysfunction then, I don't what is. But I can't make Black the scapegoat of my life. Addicts and those that have been delivered have to acknowledge their responsibility in their circumstances. As bad as Black was, he didn't control my destiny. I have to own the fact that I went out and sold my body to some of the most disgusting men and women in this world. I went out and ran scams on people to get money to support my habit. I went out and committed robberies. I, me, Bethann, went out and did those things.

Chapter Thirteen

"It was love after the fourth hit."

C rack was so powerful and destructive that in 1988 one of the top rap and political groups of all time, Chuck D and Public Enemy, released their hit song "Night of the Living Baseheads." It was a mega hit that dealt with the tragedies of crack cocaine use. Three years later the movie, "New Jack City" was released. While it was entertaining, it was one of the closest, real life depictions of the crack epidemic that was ever made.

A year later, Darryl "god" Whiting, a notorious drug kingpin from New York City, came to Boston with his crew and took over the Orchard Park Housing Projects, where I was raised as a child. They flooded our streets with crack and other illicit drugs. But crack was king and it was everywhere.

I knew crack was king after taking my fourth HIT in my living room, the first time I smoked it with Black. Back then they were still calling it freebase but whatever name it went by, it was trouble and you were in trouble if you were using it. I believe that if I had stopped after the first, second or even third hit my life would have definitely turned out differently. It's true that: *"All things work together for those of them that love the Lord and are called according to his purpose."* But that doesn't mean it was my destiny to become a crackhead. It just means that God used that situation for His glory. Sin and disobedience causes us to stray and move contrary to God and that night I chose to smoke that freebase. I signed up for the hard, long road to my destiny.

One moment I'm sitting at home in the living room with my husband, getting ready for what I thought was going to be a romantic night of lovemaking. The next moment I got a glass pipe in my mouth smoking freebase. The famous singer, Dinah Washington had a hit song named, "What a Difference a Day Makes" I'm here to tell you it made a world of difference, especially when you throw freebase cocaine into the picture. After my first night and fourth hit of freebasing, my life had changed forever and I knew it. I also knew I was in trouble. I was in love with freebasing and my appetite for that rock cocaine was unquenchable. It didn't take drugs any time to replace Black as the number one priority in my life. The reality is that Black sealed our fate when he turned me on to freebase. It was a self-fulfilling prophecy. I don't believe in Karma, but he was surely going to get what was coming to him. All the games he played and all the things he did to me actually prepared me for the journey that freebasing was getting ready to take me on. I would no longer be the student in the game. Instead, I would become the master and Black would one day regret the monster he helped create.

Within the first week, I was a full-blown base-head. Most people who decide to try freebase or crack get hooked after the first hit. It took me *four* hits, but it was still my first time trying it. Curiosity is good but please don't get so curious to ever consider trying crack. And if anybody ever offers it to you, don't walk away, run, run, like you were running for your life, because you are. That first night we freebased until I got so wasted I crashed and fell asleep. Black and I continued going hard the rest of the week until the money ran out. What was the next move? We needed to get high and we were busted. We didn't have 10 dollars between us. But Black had something in his head and up his sleeve. My hero came up with a plan, unbeknownst to me, that we would drive to a dive bar in Brockton. I knew the place, it had a bad reputation. Most people went there to either cop or sell drugs or trick.

Once we got out there, Black fell right back into his wannabe pimp ways. He passed me a handful of rubbers and told me to get out on the stroll and hustle up some money. Growing up around pimps I saw this coming a mile away. Pimps are master manipulators and play the craziest head games. They sow seeds in your mind and sell you on their pipe dreams. They touch you where you're most vulnerable, in your heart and mind, and use your weaknesses against you, all the while pretending to care about you and fronting like they want to take care of you. But his plan all along was to get me out there to sell my body for money to support our crack habit. It didn't matter how I felt or that he was placing my life in danger, I needed to get out there and get that money. Didn't he think he had done enough to me? At first I refused. But I wanted to get high and I believed that was the only way to get some money. So, I walked down the block and flagged down a couple of cars and so began my tricking career. After an hour, I had made over hundred dollars'. It was the quickest money I ever made but it came with a cost. And, Black my amazing husband, who once thought the world revolved around me and would never allow any man to even get close to me, turned me out. It wasn't enough that he got me hooked, he had to completely destroy me by turning me into a basehead ho. But I was head over heels in love with the freebase and used that whole experience to benefit myself.

After two weeks I was completely out of control. There were about four or five people in my apartment building that got high and liked to trick. I got with all of them. I was going from apartment to apartment tricking and smoking—smoking and tricking. Black, who created this monster, was not aware of all of the tricking I was doing in our apartment building. The first few times I brought the money back home and we got high together. But then I started keeping the money and going off on my own to get high.

I had one guy on the eighth floor that couldn't get enough of me. I went up there and he let me right in. He knew what I was there to do. We got right to it. This wasn't a date; I wasn't interested in talking, I was there for a business transaction, that was it. I rocked his world, he gave me the money and I was out.

Then something clicked in my head. I wasn't a great student, but I did understand simple math. And by using some simple math, I quickly realized that cocaine doesn't last as long when you have to split it with someone, especially when both of you have a crazy habit. My wannabe pimp of a husband now had a problem because he wasn't a real pimp and I was his wife, not his ho. But the bigger issue was that he needed me more than I needed him. The tables in our relationship were starting to turn. Once I figured out that I could get as much cocaine money as I needed by tricking, why did I really need him? I was the one lying on my back doing all kinds of freaky, ungodly things. So I should be the only one benefitting. I was up on the 8th floor of my building working that guy every day. I was missing from our apartment all the time and now Black was the one looking for me.

When you are getting high the way I was, things don't get better they just get worse. And true to form, things did get worse. I turned into a savage. I was prostituting with men and women and even in groups sometimes. I would let guys run trains on me as long as they all paid. I was a sex addict as much as I was a cocaine addict. My sex was so good people wanted me to trick with them, their boyfriends, girlfriends, and their husbands and wives. Yes, I tricked with married people on many occasions. The ironic part about that scenario is that it wasn't my first time engaging in threesomes and foursomes. I had experience with that from going to the extreme to try and keep Black at home and satisfied. He suggested spicing up our marriage by having a threesome. I wanted to keep my marriage so bad that I asked one of my girlfriends, who liked me and Black, to join us in our bedroom. She was all too willing to participate. He became more interested in her over me and acted like I wasn't in the room. Black had a thing for my girlfriend. In my attempt to keep the marriage, I ended up being the loser. It seemed like every situation I got involved in with Black I came out on the losing end.

Both Black and I were out of control. Cocaine was literally driving us to think and act reckless and irrational. Feigning for the rock drove me insane. As I said before, I was so desperate and irresponsible that while feigning for drugs, I had unprotected sex with a guy who the streets said had AIDS. That tells you how much I wanted to get high. The rumor in the streets was true. He did have AIDS, and he died not long after we had sex. That didn't stop me. Nothing could stop me. I was strung out and things just kept getting crazier. Imagine a crazy life like this all while trying to raise a son.

Chapter Fourteen

"The first hit of it is like nothing else. The world sort of just stops. It's got this sweet taste to it. It's very hard to describe..."
Richard Preston

Crack will make you pull some amazing stunts. I could literally write a book just about all the stunts I pulled during my 30 year battle with the drug. Each year I got more sophisticated with my hustles. I ran so many different scams on family and businesses such as stores, law firms, hospitals, you name it. If there was money to be had, I went out and got it. I made big scores in the thousands and even tens of thousands of dollars. I had a crazy hustle along with my crazy habit. But all crackheads are resourceful. If you ever had a run in with a crackhead you know where I'm coming from. They can tell the most amazing stories and if they catch you slippin', you will fall for their game. A serious crackhead will break into your house, steal you television and then try and sell it back to you. They will steal your drugs or money and then help you look for it. Crackheads have some of the most creative minds in the world.

Chasing a crack high will also lead you to put your loved ones in danger. You don't care about the consequences as long as you can get high. For years I put some of my closest family members, including my son, in harm's way. Black and I, totally strung out and trying to care for our young son, would run all kinds of scams. Just saying that aloud sounds crazy. But we were out of our minds.

We had plenty of near death experiences while we were crack addicts. I remember one time Black beat this Dominican drug dealer, Papi, for like a half ounce of coke. They had made a deal to trade some coke for Black's gold chain. So one day they met up and made the deal. I didn't think much about it. In the street you are always making deals like that. A few days later someone slides a tarnished gold chain under our door. So now a red flag is going off in my head. What the heck is this about? Black tells me that it was the chain he traded with Papi for the coke. I'm like "You traded him a fake chain?" I thought the chain was real. "All this time you been walking around like you had a real chain." Now I'm getting concerned because I know the type of guy Papi is. Sure enough, about a week later Papi knocked on our door looking for Black. I was scared because those Dominican dudes were known for killing people over a little bit of money and we were talking about a few hundred dollars. Papi was pissed, and this wasn't going to end well and Black knew it.

Black decided to skip town for a while. He took our son and went to Detroit to stay with some of his family. About a week later Papi came back looking for his money. I didn't want any drama with that man. I knew what he was capable of. I told him the truth that Black left town because he didn't have his money and was scared he might be killed. Black burned that bridge with Papi and almost got killed in the process. But that's how things happen in the streets when you are smoking crack all the time. You become completely reckless. That's what we had become. And in the midst of it all, I was still desperately seeking a hero.

Black would tell stories I knew were lies, but I wanted to believe him so bad. After beating Papi, Black called me from Detroit with some story about a car he found. He said it was a pretty Cadillac that would be a nice family car. He said he wanted to get the car for "US." I guess us meant him. But I got the money together and sent it to him. His plan was to buy the car then drive back to Boston with our son. I think deep down inside I knew the Cadillac story was a lie but hoped it was true. Also, a lot of times crack addicts have good intentions but the drugs take over. Maybe he really planned to buy it, until he got the money in hand. Either way, I wanted him to be back with me and as silly as it might sound, I wanted us to be a family again. I knew he was getting high so I wasn't going to send the money to him directly. I sent the money to his grandmother to hold. Still hoping things were going to work out, I waited a while to see what was really up. Had Black played me for some money again? Did Black smoke it all up? Black was ghost so I had to get to the bottom of it. I hadn't heard a word after I sent the money. After a few days, I called his grandmother to see what was happening. She was like, "Girl he done got that money and I haven't seen him for three days." I realized he had talked his grandmother out of the money and went and smoked it up. I was devastated, but I shouldn't have been. He was a crackhead, just like me and that's what we do, lie, deceive, disappoint and damage everything we come in contact with while we're using. Yet, I still had to confront him face to face. It was a major sacrifice to get that money. I was babysitting my sister's daughter at the time. I tried calling my sister to come and get her baby because I had to leave town immediately. I couldn't find my sister so I took the baby and we hopped on the next flight headed to Detroit. I had an idea of where he was. I found him and just like I knew, he had smoked up all the money I sent him for the car. I should have just left him right where he was and took my son with me. But naïve me still had a little hope for us. I looked him in his eyes and said, "If you can just show me one penny, I'll forgive you and take you back." He didn't have one red cent left. I really should have left him. But I didn't have money to get back to Boston. We had to stay in Detroit to accumulate enough money to get back. I still had my sister's new baby with me. To earn money, I hustled a bit with my cough medicine game plus I had my worker's compensation checks coming in. Black managed to steal the money I would bring in. It took me five months to get us all back home. By the time we got back to Boston, my sister's baby was walking and potty trained. Reluctantly, I brought Black back home to Boston where we got an apartment right outside of town. We had to start over, but we had a few schemes going and ending up getting a settlement. However, as soon as we got the money we smoked it up. With every piece of money we got, no matter how big or small, we smoked it up. Every time we got kicked out of one apartment we would turn the next one into a crack house. We did that a number of times, with our son, until we were finally homeless.

We sent our son to my grandmother's to live. I felt bad but that was the best for him. We couldn't really give him the stability and structure he needed. When both parents are strung out, the child suffers. I don't try and minimize the damage I caused my son. I did the best a crack addict could do. I don't know how, but I still managed to make sure he had everything he needed. When I first started getting high, one of my girlfriends taught me how to boost. I became a master booster. So I went downtown to some of the nice department stores and stole all kinds of clothes and sneakers for my son as well as clothes to sell for crack.

Black was so impressed by my boosting skills he wanted me to keep going. One store we hit so many times that the people figured out I was stealing but could never catch me. I wanted to slow down but Black wanted to keep hitting them. He kept pressing me and I kept going until one day one of the staff caught me. They brought me to the security office of the store and had me wait until the police arrived. They said, "We know you got something, where is it?" I played stupid. When they left me alone in the room, I took all the stolen stuff off of me and threw it in the corner of their office. The police came and they questioned me about where the stuff was. Then the store's security guard looked over at the corner of the room and saw the stuff and said, "There it goes, I knew she was shoplifting." I started to make a big scene, declaring I didn't have that stuff. Instead I switched up on them by saying the people in the store were trying to set me up. I told the police I didn't have anything to do with that stuff and the people are harassing me and I would get a lawyer to sue them. We went back and forth for a few minutes until the police asked the store security, "Can you prove she took the stuff?" They couldn't prove it and had to let me go. Back then, they didn't have cameras everywhere. Nevertheless, that was another situation Black got me into for his selfish reasons. He never cared about my feelings or safety. He only cared about what I could do for him.

I can't say that it was all bad with Black, but after several years of his chaotic mess, I was ready to move on. Plenty of men wanted to be with me and I was still confident I'd eventually find my hero.

Chapter Fifteen

"Good riddance to bad news."

Life is funny. I have always believed that everything happens for a reason, and everything happens in due season. I don't believe in coincidences. Black and I were done. I was finished with him and would have been happy to never see him again. Unfortunately, I wouldn't be so lucky or should I say, blessed. We would later have a run-in that still haunts me to this day. However, I don't allow him any space in my spirit. Anyways, I had moved on from Black and he became a non-factor in my life. Then one day the strangest thing happened. My phone rang, I picked it up, and it was a wrong number. But instead of just hanging up the phone, I engaged with the person on the other line. He thought he dialed the right number, and I was the girlfriend of the guy he was trying to reach. The craziest part of the call is that I actually knew the person he was trying to reach. So he really thought I was trying to play on the phone. So finally I told him, "Look you called the wrong number, but I know Bobby and I know why you called him. So how long have you been getting high?" He laughed and said, "Quit playing and put Bobby on the phone." I told him again: "This is not Bobby's phone. Take my number, hang up and dial the number you thought you dialed and see what happens." He did it and then realized that he, in fact, had called the wrong number. He called me right back and later that day we met up.

When we met in person, I immediately saw how handsome he was, and younger, a lot younger than me. He didn't look much older than my son. I guess you could say I was on my "cougar grind" because I was definitely feeling him. We had great chemistry, well to keep it 100, as the kids say, the sex was off the chain. You had me hooked if the sex was good. I had multiple addictions and sex was one of them. I just seemed to naturally gravitate to you if the sex was good. I'm not ashamed to say our thing was purely sexual. It worked for me at the time and it was way less stressful and more fun than dealing with Black. However, Trevor's immaturity didn't take long to show up. I think he had some mental health issues too. Here I go again with another wannabe. This one didn't wannabe a pimp he wanted to be a thug. He liked to fight and had a big mouth. The only thing was he couldn't back up the trash he talked. But I still chilled with him because, like I said, the sex was crazy. However, after a while you have to bring more to the table than sex. I was a grown woman with worldly experience. I had seen more and lived more than Trevor and good sex only lasts so long. A few months into our relationship, Trevor crossed the line and decided that he would put his hands on me. What is it with all these men thinking it's okay to hit a woman? I wonder if it was because I smoked crack and that meant I wasn't worthy of respect. Regardless, I was back into another abusive relationship. One day Trevor came over to my house and wanted to take me and my son out for ice cream. While we were walking to the store, we got into an argument about something really silly. He slapped me in public, in front of my son. I was livid and ready to fight, but I didn't. Believe it or not, Black was looking out the window of his sidechick's apartment and witnessed the whole thing. He came down to where we were and grabbed Trevor. Black swung on Trevor and missed. Trevor ran like the punk he was. Black took me and our son to his friend, Slick's, house, and we ended up getting back together again. But our relationship was so toxic that it didn't last long. Soon he was gone, Trevor was gone and I was fine with it all. But I have to give Black credit for showing up, at least that time anyways. And Trevor turned out to be more of a boy than a man.

I forgave Trevor. I had a forgiving heart when it came to the men in my life. We got back together again for a while. I just knew he was a punk who couldn't fight and I accepted it. Although all his tough talk annoyed me, I dealt with it for a while until the day I desperately needed him to help me, and he didn't step up. I had a scam that I worked out with one of my old landlords. It was against the federal government and there is no statute of limitations with the feds so I have to tread very carefully. Anyways, every third of the month my ex landlord would give me a payment. I had a routine that I strictly followed. I would pick up the payment, then go see my dealer and buy a bunch of crack. I didn't deviate from that routine. The problem with routines is that people who are close to you learn them, and if they have bad intentions, they can hurt you. And that's exactly what happened to me one day. I had gone to meet the ex-landlord and picked up the money. I hid the money because the lifestyle I lived people were always trying to rob and steal from each other. People devised schemes to set others up. It was just another part of that life. Anyways, I had jumped on the bus and headed towards the dealer's house. Low and behold, Black and his boy, Slick, were hiding across the street from the dealer's house, waiting for me to show up. As I got close to the stairs of the building, someone ran up and punched me in the back of the head. It was Black. He was with his boy, Slick. Trevor yelled out to them, "I'm calling the police." Black shouted, Where's the money B?" I told him I didn't have any money. Black and Slick beat me up bad. They must have punched me in my face and head 10 times. They threw me to the ground and were kicking me, bruising my ribs pretty bad. They went through my pockets and couldn't find the money. I had put it below, in my secret stash spot. They ran off empty handed. I was beaten badly, but I still had my money. Trevor never moved off the porch and watched as two men nearly killed me. All his trash talking, he never moved. But I knew what he was. I knew he wasn't built for this life and I knew that was it for us. I went to my grandmother's, and she was so upset. She called my uncle and told him to call his boys and my other family and go find Black and break both of his legs. But Black got wind of it and skipped town. They said he went to Chicago. It's a good thing because they were going to seriously hurt him. My grandmother had a little gangster in her. I stayed at her house for a few days to heal. I looked a mess. I mean my face was swollen and I was almost unrecognizable. But that wasn't enough for me to stop getting high. But it was enough for me to cut ties with Black forever and send Trevor back to the sandbox I found him in. The two of them together didn't equal a half of a man.

My hero was out there and I was determined to find him.

Chapter Sixteen

"I was savage when it came to men. They come
in and out of my life like a revolving door."

Two bad apples don't spoil the whole bunch and two losers couldn't make me give up on trying to find Mr. Right. You know the old saying, "If at first you don't succeed try, try, again." Well, that's exactly what I did over and over again until the Lord saved me and told me to stand still in my relationship with my current husband.

I had so many different men in my life. I dealt with three or four men at a time. I had them on strings like I was a puppet master. I used and manipulated them for my pleasure and to get what I needed. That was a lifetime ago and I thank God for my deliverance.

Before I started getting high, I was a one man woman. I wanted the story book marriage and life. I used to call myself a hopeless romantic. But all that changed when I said "I do." My first husband crushed all my dreams of a happily ever after. He nearly destroyed my life after he got me strung out. His manipulative and controlling ways turned me into a hardened savage. I learned to move methodically, turning the tables on him and every other man that tried to rule, control or abuse me. I became the master manipulator at using men. In fact, I earned a Ph.D. in getting what I wanted and needed. Sex was my main tool, but it was my thinking ability that allowed me to stay alive on the streets for so long. I used to love having sex and most men I met in that world did too. When the money and the drugs ran out, I always had something to offer. Tricking was a big part of getting high. And you would be surprised by the things men will do for sex. Tricks are all the same. I don't care what walk of life they come from. They are doctors, lawyers, policemen, judges or garbage men, you name it. There is an abundance of them out there willing to pay money for sex. If you were as good at it, as I was, they came looking for you. When you're desperate for that fix, you will do whatever. I have to keep saying it over and over; the life of a crack addict is terrible. It's 100 times worse than what you see on television and in the movies. You are not living, you are just existing and conforming or transforming into whatever character you have to be in order to get your next high.

After completely cutting ties with both Black and Trevor, I was out on the streets. I was back at it again, doing my thing, flopping in crack houses and making money anyway I could. I walked up into one crack house and who do I see across the room getting high, Chester. He was one of my most toxic flings. I really had no business messing with Chester, and I never would have if crack was not involved. I'm sure you can imagine why I call him Chester. Chester was one of my stepfather's pimping friends who I used to babysit for as a teenager. We really had no business messing around with each other, but that's how it goes down in the crack game. But again, as I said previously, men, especially unsaved men, will be men.

We hooked up one night and the sex was bananas. The sex is the only reason I really dealt with him for almost 13 years. Anyways, that night I saw him in the crack house, we went to his sister's and stayed together in her basement. I had a good time. After a few days, I went back to my house in Everett. He was sprung and wanted me to come back and stay with him. He was really feeling me so I decided why not. So I went and stayed with him. He thought he was slick. He was trying to groom me to get me out on the track to support our habit. A pimp is a creature of habit. He is always thinking of ways to get a girl out on the track to make some money for him. I knew Chester was running game, but so was I. We were just two crackheads trying to figure out our next lick (score).

One night while cooking dinner I got real sick. I had to go home to my house. I went there to rest and relax and hopefully get better. However, I got worse and ended up almost fainting. My aunt rushed me to the hospital and they admitted me. They ran several tests and diagnosed me with parasites. I had been sleeping in that basement and it wasn't the greatest place to live. The doctor thought perhaps I contracted the parasites from some dirty water. But I knew that wasn't the case. My system was made out of steel. In the past, I had eaten out of all kinds of crack houses and they were not the cleanest. In fact they were nasty and dirty. Whatever the case, it's a good thing I made it to the hospital when I did. I was dying and didn't even know it. My system was all messed up and my electrolyte balance was dangerously out of whack. I'm pretty sure my illness was caused from the drugs I was smoking, but I wouldn't tell that to the doctors who were treating me. Whatever it was, it was bad. They kept me for two weeks. And still, after all of that, I wanted to get high. I actually did once or twice.

Chester was playing the role of a concerned and caring boyfriend. I shouldn't be so cynical. Maybe he really did care in some sick, distorted way. He came up to the hospital every day to visit. Sometimes he would even drive my mother home afterwards. He did a good job of making me think he really cared. But the drugs had me going crazy. I was so delusional that I actually thought my mother was after him. When you use so many drugs as I did, you become super paranoid and can't think rationally. It happened to me quite a few times. It's a terrible feeling. My mother wasn't thinking about Chester, she was just a loving person. The hospital stay turned out to be a blessing in disguise. I got some well needed rest. I was relatively clean and my head was clear. I decided to try and get my act together. My younger sister had offered me a part time job so I took her up on the offer.

However, as soon as I got out of the hospital, I went right to my grandmother's to pick up my three worker's comp checks and went straight to the drug dealer. I bought a whole bunch of coke and smoked it all. It made me sick because I was still weak from the hospital stay. About two weeks later, I started working. I was trying to do the right thing and not get high. I gave the money I was getting from the little part time plus my worker's comp checks to Chester's sister to hold. I knew I couldn't be trusted with money. She was no nonsense and wasn't giving me the money back until I needed it for bills or to take care of my responsibilities. I was taking care of business and I was proud of myself. Things seemed to be going a lot better.

Chester was so nice that when I got out of the hospital I tried to make things work with him. We devised a plan to purchase a house and use my

Section 8 subsidy to pay the mortgage. It was a great plan in theory, however, completely impossible for two crackheads. Still we tried. While I was focused and working, Chester and his buddy were sitting around our apartment getting high every day. His buddy had come into some money, and they were blowing through it fast. They were coming down to the last of the money when they went into "fiend scheming" mode. Most crackheads are always scheming and thinking about how they are going to get more money or drugs. One day when I came home from work, Chester and his buddy were in the living room. I walked in and saw a table full of cocaine and three glass pipes. And they were not one for the Father, one for the Son and one for the Holy Ghost. There was one for Chester, one for his friend, Michael, and one for me. Thanks, guys! This was the ultimate setup. Here I was trying my hardest to do the right thing and get my life in order. I hadn't been that focused and disciplined in a long time. I had truly been working to stay clean, and I had to walk into a trap that was sent straight from the pits of hell. Those two had no idea that they were being used as instruments of Satan. They set me up.

Cocaine had been out of sight and out of mind for me. As long as I stayed away from the stuff, I was fine. I walked into that living room and just sat down and cried, asking them "Why are you doing this to me? You know you are getting ready to create a monster even bigger than I was before."

Addiction is an evil spirit and the crack demon had been locked away in a closet for a little while. But these guys knew what they were doing. They planned to use me to feed their habit because they were running out of money. They didn't care that I was on the verge of messing up my life again. They wanted me back getting high so they could get to that money I had put away. I'm not going to say I was helpless, but I wasn't delivered. One thing I'm pretty confident of is that I probably wouldn't have gotten high as long as I wasn't around the drugs. I was getting better and stronger every day as long as I stayed away from it. But if you dangle cheese in front of a mouse or if you dangle carrots in front of a rabbit, you know what's going to happen. The same thing happens when you put a fully loaded crack pipe in front of a crackhead. I took the pipe and once I put it to my lips, that was it. We got high all night. And I never went back to work.

Again, I chose my addiction. Once the stuff was gone, I went through all the money that I had worked so hard to save. I was strung out again and in worse shape than before, with no money.

Chester told me to go out with one of his pimping friend's girls. She had a hook-up at their Hilton Hotel at the Airport, and I made over $700 the first night. I was tired went to bed, and the next day we were off to the races. We smoked that money up right away. I started doing the math again and realized after a while that I no longer needed Chester. I took Chester's car and was out doing all kinds of stuff to get high. I went looking for Tony, he was a dealer who liked me and liked to smoke. I ended up staying with him for like five days. I went back home to Chester and things didn't get any better, they never do. Throughout our time together, Chester and I kept pulling stunts and getting settlements. However, no matter how much money we came into, it never lasted. A lot of what we experienced was written in the Book of Haggai 1:6: "*Ye have sown much, and bring in little; ye eat, but ye have not enough; ye drink, but ye are not filled with drink; ye clothe you, but there is none warm; and he that earneth*

wages earneth wages to put it into a bag with holes."
One day Chester got stopped for driving without a
license. The car was impounded. It was only a $45
fine, but we were so into getting high that we didn't
pay it. The storage fees kept adding up until it was
some outrageous amount and we ended up losing the
car. Then we got a car from my brother. The car had a
$99 monthly payment. We never paid it, and the car
was repossessed. Then his mother gave us a car. We
didn't make the payment and lost that car.

Any money we came into, we smoked up. Both of
us got steadily worse. Then one day we were shooting
up cocaine and I went into convulsions. I was
overdosing and in danger of dying. Chester and his
friend didn't call the paramedics. They picked me up
and started to carry me outside to throw me away in
the back yard like trash. Instead, the Lord had plans
for my life and sent an angel, in the form of my
brother. Before Chester and his friend even made it to
the door with me, unexpectedly, my brother was
ringing the bell. They told him that I had just
overdosed, and somehow he brought me back. Let's
not leave out that Chester and his boy also stole the
rest of the cocaine and the money I had on me. I

almost died that night, and my man was ready to leave me for dead, and that's pretty sad. However, what's even sadder is that same night, after almost dying from an overdose, I regained consciousness and immediately went back and got the rest of my cocaine and shot up again. Chester then started going off on his own, smoking without me, so I got angry. As time went on,. I got fed up and took my Section 8 voucher and moved out of the apartment we shared. I had to be in control. But at the end of the day I was not.

Chapter Seventeen

"The best way to manipulate a man is to
make him think he is manipulating you."
John Smith

Throughout my 30-year battle with crack cocaine, so many different men came through my life. My bedroom was like a revolving door. After my first marriage, I was never monogamous until I got saved. Most of the time, I dealt with at least two or three men at a time. It was an amazing juggling act that I mastered. I ran cons on them all. Convincing multiple men to pay child support for children that didn't even exist was just evil. But that was the life I led.

I had to get away from Chester for a while. All the fighting and drama got to be too much for me. Chester was like a jealous woman following me around like Oran "Juice" Jones trying to keep tabs on me. He knew what our relationship was. He knew how I hustled. Why was he walking around camouflaging himself like he was a soldier fighting in Iraq, while spying on me? They should have taken away his pimp card for that type of behavior. After I moved out, Chester started acting more crazy. He was stalking me on the streets and trying to break into my house. He actually got in a few times. He was like a super ninja crackhead the way he scaled the roof of the building and climbed into my third floor bedroom window. Then he would hide in a closet and wait to see who I would trick within the apartment. They say you never miss a good thing until it's gone. And I was a good thing and I was gone and Chester wanted me back. Someone might ask, "How can you be a crackhead and a good thing at the same time?" Was I just delusional and we were simply two co-dependent addicts who needed and deserved one another?

I was unsaved and controlled by multiple demons. I had done so much crack that I became a paranoid mess. I thought the police and the FBI were after me. I needed a safe place to stay. About a month later, I decided to return to Chester's house. We picked right up from where we left off and fought a lot. He was crazy possessive and began following me again. I wasn't paranoid about him following me. And it didn't stop me from doing my thing.

Chester got into a situation with some people and was beaten up badly. His injuries were so severe that he went into a rehab center for a few weeks. I was glad. Not glad that he got beat up but happy he was out of my hair for a little while. I needed the break from him.

I was out again chasing down cars on the Ave., turning tricks to maintain my habit and unbeknownst to me someone else was watching me. His name was Mister. He was a big time drug dealer who had much respect around the way. He was a square. He didn't get high, he just dealt. One day he finally approached me. We had good chemistry and instantly connected. I invited him over to Chester's' house that night. Chester was gone so I basically had the house to myself. It was kind of a slimy move, but I wanted to get with him and my addiction was calling the shots. We had sex that night in me and Chester's bed. We had to be cool because my son and his girlfriend were in the other room. The next night I went to his house. We started getting together every night. I became his eleven o'clock booty call. But Mister was different, he was a keeper. I didn't feel like I was tricking when I was with him. Soon we went from that eleven o'clock booty call to having real feelings for each other. He was my "Boo Thang" and he made sure it was known. He told everybody I was his woman and not to mess with me. It was kind of a blessing in disguise. Now I didn't have to go out in the streets and trick and steal because I could get as much crack as I wanted from him. Maybe this was as close to a hero that I was going to get. He was a real man who loved me and wanted to protect me. I felt safe and secure with Mister. But my addiction wouldn't allow me to rest easy with him. A crackhead can't be true to a real loving relationship. The drugs will not allow you to remain loyal and faithful to anyone but them. They become your master. They speak to all of your weaknesses, fears, and lusts as soon as anyone attempts to take their place in your life. Mister tried to replace them. He started by trying to control the amount I used. That was his biggest mistake. The drugs kicked my mind into scheme mode and it was all downhill for us from that point. He didn't even see it coming. He couldn't. He didn't get high. Part of the crack addition is more. The more you use, the more you want. So if Mister wasn't going to keep giving me more, than I would go out and get it myself. His feelings and my loyalty to him meant nothing any longer. It was all about me and my number one love, my crack addiction and no one could replace it. It sent me back out tricking. I didn't need Mister to get high. I was getting high before I met him and I would still be getting high after him.

Anyways, I started tricking again. I would be out for days at a time, and Mister had no idea where I was. He would put the word out that if anyone sees Beth he had something for them. He had spies. Some would warn me and others would let him know where they saw me. I don't blame them because I would have given them up too for some crack. I learned the hard way to always be 100 steps in front of my situation. My mind was always working and planning. I was 100 steps ahead of any one I was dealing with and they had no idea.

One night while Mister and I were having sex, the condom broke. He was shook, and I saw it all over his face. I had him. He was like hurry up and go in the bathroom and take a douche. I refused. I started acting really angry and told him he messed up because I get pregnant easy. A few weeks later I came back and told him I was pregnant. He was like you need to go get an abortion, and he gave me the money. I wasn't pregnant, but I was going to take advantage of his mess up. Sometimes I couldn't believe how gullible he was. After that I must have played the "I am pregnant" game on him 20 times. Each and every time he gave me money for an abortion. He was clueless when it came to my hustles. I took it to the next level since that game was working so well on him. I decided to tell him I was pregnant and keeping the baby. He was upset but paid me child support for years. I had him thinking he had a total of five kids, a set of triplets, set of twins and another one. I told him one of the triplets died during birth. I made up all kinds of crazy, elaborate stories. I even named the kids. He took care of all five of them. I told him some of the kids were taken by DSS, while the others were with my family in another state. That game went on for many years. His family would tell him I was playing him, but he loved me and believed everything I said. Whenever he stopped believing me or seemed skeptical, I would pull another stunt. Sometimes it took days for me to devise a plan. I feel like I truly loved him, but in the end, I beat him just like I beat everybody else in my life. There were so many times I could have done the right thing, but I just couldn't.

Chapter Eighteen

*"Beloved, while I was very diligent to write to you
concerning our common salvation, I found it
necessary to write to you to contend earnestly for the
faith which was once for all delivered to the saints."*
Jude 1:3

I have been involved with church, off and on, since
I was a teenager. I have been saved a number of
times and backslid. I don't believe the once in
doctrine because I know that with the things I've done,
I could no longer be saved. Until I was completely
delivered, I was just going through the motions and
expressing a form of Godliness, yet denying the power.
And when you are battling the spirit of addiction, you
need the whole armor of God. The Apostle Paul said:
"Put on the whole armour of God that ye may be able to

stand against the wiles of the devil." I remember one of the times I decided to get saved. I started going back to church. I had been hitting the streets hard and I needed a rest. The streets beat you down, you get tired after a while and crash. My mother had taken me in and I was really trying to get myself together. I started going to church regularly and felt like I was getting stronger.

I stopped using completely and things in my life were better. My head was clearer and I was making better decisions. I decided to have my checks deposited into my mother's bank account because I was still weak with money and honestly didn't trust myself. I had been getting high long enough to know that money was a trigger for me. Having money on me caused my body to change. I would get an uneasy feeling in my stomach and be ready to find my dealer. It didn't have to be a lot of money, just $10 and I would start thinking about where to go grab a rock.

One day we got a call that my brother was caught dealing drugs. My mother was distraught. She wanted him out of jail right away. Like I told you before, her kids were her life and she would always come for us, no matter the situation. I had stolen from her several times and she never stopped loving and praying for me. When the family told her to disown me, she just prayed and petitioned the Lord on my behalf. At this time, I was clean and had built up some trust with my mother. She told me I would have to go bail out my brother. She went down to her bank, withdrew $3,500 and trustfully handed it to me. I was supposed to take the money down to the jail and meet up with my brother's friend who had the rest of the $20,000 bail. I went to my brother's house and grabbed some of his clothes to bring him. But his clothes had the scent of crack on them, which caused my stomach to start turning. How could this be? I was going to church, had stopped using and thought my addiction was behind me. Boy, was I was completely wrong. I jumped on the bus. While on the bus, the crack demon began speaking to me. Demons are very tricky. Oftentimes they lay dormant waiting for the right opportunity to present themselves. Well, this was the perfect time because I had a pocket full of money, along with crack residue filling my nose. The Bible describes the enemy as a roaring lion travelling to and fro seeking who to devour. It challenged me to see if I was really delivered.

I wasn't. The devil convinced me to go buy a $10 bump and see if I could stop at one. Just for the record, there is no crackhead walking around with $3,500 in their pocket who can simply go get a $10 hit and stop.

As I said before, a crack habit is an addiction of "more." The crack high wears off so quickly that you are constantly chasing that next one. Needless to say, I jumped off the bus and went by one of my dealer's houses and brought a $10 hit. Nothing else mattered now except getting high. I didn't think about my brother getting out of jail or the betrayal to my beloved mother. After I took that hit, the race was on; $3,490 of my mother's money was on its way to the next drug dealer. Another regret!

To make matters worse, my ex-husband, Black, was at that house. When he realized I had a lot of money, he decided to play the concerned husband role. Never in our relationship was he ever truly concerned about me. He was only concerned about what I could do for him. Black decided he wanted to hold the money to protect it from getting stolen. I knew he was up to no good. I've seen all his games and flimflams. He kept asking me for the money, but I wouldn't give it to him. I was thinking of ways to keep him from getting the rest of the money. There was about $1,500 left at this point. We went to his mother's house to stay for the night. I racked my brain trying to find a good hiding spot, but there was no safe place in that house. Finally, I decided the best idea was to put the money in a baggie and place it up inside my lady parts. That hiding spot didn't work. When I woke the next day, my concerned ex-husband, Black, and what was left of the money was gone. I was vexed. Now I had to go find him. It didn't take long because I knew he would be at one of two places. I found him and he didn't want to give me the money back. He wanted to control the situation and tell me how we were going to spend the money. I was so mad that he violated me like that. I wanted to slice his throat. But the most important thing was for me to get that money back. That money was running out fast. I only had like $1,500 left. So I went into game mode and came up with a plan. I said to Black, "Let's go over to Deedee's house so we can pool our money together to buy some coke and flip it." We went to my friend, Deedee's house and devised a plan to make a big drug deal. We needed the $1,500 of my money that Black was still holding. Then Deedee was going to put in some money. I made Black believe I had more money to complete the drug deal. He was stalling at first. I was telling him to hurry up because the Puerto Rican kid was coming with the stuff. He gave me the money. I went into Deedee's bedroom and told her, "Alright I got the money back, now put him out." Deedee went into the living room and told him to get out. Deedee pulled out her knife. I grabbed her bat and told him if he didn't leave we would kill him. All of sudden he became remorseful and acted as if he was trying to help me. He asked why I was doing this to him and he didn't have any money. I told him: "You didn't have any money when we met up. You took my money and bounced and wasn't thinking about me. Get out." Then the man, who was once my hero, my superman started to cry. He had nowhere to go and it was in the middle of a snowstorm. It felt good having the power for once. Watching him walk out the door was poetic justice.

I still smoked up the rest of the money, but it was on my terms. However, I was now worse than ever. My addiction was out of control. The Bible says: *"When an impure spirit comes out of a person, it goes through arid places seeking rest and does not find it. Then it says "I will return to the house I left." When it arrives, it finds the house unoccupied, swept clean and put in order. Then it goes and takes with it seven other spirits more wicked than itself, and they go in and live there. And the final condition of that person is worse than the first."* That scripture is so true. After being saved and then backsliding, I was a bigger crackhead than I had ever been.

Over and over for years, things like this happened. It's hard for people who never battled a major drug addiction to believe people lived like I did. I have hundreds of stories like this. Nothing changed until that one day when the light came on. Something told me I had to make a change or my life would be over.

Chapter Nineteen

*"Cast all your anxiety on Him
because He cares for you."*
1 Peter 5:7

God miraculously removed some of my greatest sins and weights once I accepted Him into my life. Things that were impossible for me to do on my own, God removed. But it wasn't easy and it wasn't overnight. The deliverance process was tough and almost cost me my sanity. One of the biggest things that weighed me down and tormented me even after my deliverance was guilt. Guilt can kill you if you allow it to fester.

I hadn't seen my mother in seven months. I was ducking her hard. She would call on the phone and I would look at the Caller ID and just let it ring. Sometimes she would let the phone ring 20 or 30 times. Caller ID was like an insurance policy for addicts because 90 percent of your calls were people looking for you because you owed them money or you beat them for some drugs. When you get high as I did, people are always looking to get in touch with you. Back then, I didn't know anything about social media, so there were only two ways for someone to reach me, either by phone or to come to my house. You had total control over whether you wanted to make yourself available. The addiction had me out of control and my mother knew it. When I didn't answer her calls, she would have my brothers and sisters try to reach me. I didn't answer anyone. When I didn't answer, they would show up at my house and try and catch me off guard. However I wouldn't answer the door either. My life had gotten so bad that I didn't want anyone to see me, especially my mother. Other family members tried different ways to reach me as well, but I didn't fall for any of it. I had the mind of a crackhead and slick stuff I could see a mile away. I knew how to lay low and disappear if needed.

On August 4, 2004, it was near the first of the month, and all the crack fiends had money. The SSI checks had come and like clockwork we all stayed up smoking until we ran out of money. However, this time I fell asleep before all the drugs were gone. I was knocked out in my bedroom. Me and my girl, Betty, had been on a five-day crack binge and I finally crashed. I don't know how she was still going. Every bit of energy I had left my body. While I was sleeping, I felt someone brush against my feet. I jumped up, looked around and no one was there. Then I remembered leaving Betty in the living room. Maybe it was her. I got up and she was still on the couch, hitting that pipe hard, so it wasn't her who touched me. Since I was up, I started hitting the pipe again. About two hours later I got the call that changed my life, "Mama's dead." It was my youngest brother on the phone. I didn't believe him. I thought it was a ploy they came up with to get me to go see my mother. "You're buggin', don't play like that," I told my brother. But then things started to get real. A little while later, my niece came by the house, knocked on my door and said, "Nana's dead." I told her not to believe that story, it's a lie. I told her to go to the hospital and see for herself. My niece went down and confirmed that my mother had passed away. How could this be? I fell apart. My mother, who I hadn't seen or talked to for several months, was really dead. The crackhead in me rose up. All I could think about was using my mother's death to get sympathy from the drug dealers. As my mother's dead body lay on the cold, steel slab in the basement morgue of the Beth Israel Hospital, I was yet scheming for my next lick. If that's not sick, then tell me what is? If there is anything worse than pathetic, that's what I was. This was the time I was supposed to be there for my mother, like all the times she'd been there for me. She was gone, my family needed me and all I could do was get high. Each hit chipped away at the mountain of guilt I was dealing with. So I just kept smoking until I was able to deal with myself. My family handled her Homegoing Service. I just showed up. On the day of the service, I stood by the casket, still thinking that they were trying to trick me. I was high and buggin'. She didn't even look like my mother lying in that box. I turned and looked at the congregation and began cursing them all out. I remember telling them that this was the lowest joke they could ever play. I was enraged. I said, "Where is my F-ing mother?" I said a few more choice words and ran out of the church. I had finally snapped to the point of possibly not being able to come back to reality. Some of the people in the congregation followed me outside to the parking lot and began to pray for me. These people were for real. They went to the throne of grace in that parking lot, interceding for me. They touched heaven, and I was able to go back inside. However, all I could think about was getting a hit of crack. My mother is laying here dead and her death couldn't even stop the addiction, not even for five minutes. That thing had complete control of me. I was at my worst. I stood by her casket feigning for another hit, and I wouldn't allow anyone to get close to her. I thought about the missed phone calls and hiding behind the curtains when she came by to see me. I couldn't wait to get out of there and go smoke. I wanted to try and put this whole situation behind me. And just when I didn't think things could get any worse, a few days later my grandmother (my mother's mother), passed away. I was sleeping, and again I felt something brush against my feet. I believe that was both Nana's and my mother's way of letting me know they had gone on, and I needed to step up. But I didn't, because I was too busy getting high. I never even made it to my grandmother's funeral. I felt worthless and sorry for myself. Instead of trying to get clean, I took getting high to yet another level. People in recovery will tell you that as long as you're getting high, things won't get better, they can only get worse. Just when you think you've hit rock bottom, the floor opens up and there is a new low waiting for you. And if you continue on, you either sink to that new low or you die.

The guilt seemed like it was too much to bear. I had to live with myself knowing I was not there when my mother died. I never got to tell her thanks or that I loved her or to even say goodbye. It haunted me. The guilt consumed me. I started thinking about my son and how I wasn't there for him in his time of need. He was in prison getting the news about his "Mama," that's what he called his grandmother. There would be no one there to comfort him. I had so many emotions inside of me and I was mad at the world. They had taken away the three people I loved the most. I suppressed my feelings and turned into a heartless beast who didn't care about anyone or anything.

Everyone who crossed my path got it. I was on a collision course with death and I really didn't care. I even contemplated suicide. However if I did that, I wouldn't be able to get high any longer. How sick was that, not wanting to commit suicide because I'd no longer be able to get high. I was completely gone to the point of no return, so I thought. But God specializes in hopeless, lost causes and He had a plan for my life.

Chapter Twenty

*"If we confess our sins, He is faithful and just to forgive
us our sins, to cleanse us from all unrighteousness."*
1 John 1:9

After my mother's passing and the devastation of my life that ensued, it took me another six long, miserable years to come out of that horrible pit of despair my life had become. The process was awful and I had no idea if I'd ever make it out. I had no hope in my chances, and I lost faith in God. But God in His infinite wisdom was working things out on my behalf. In the Book of Matthew 11:28 it reads: *Then Jesus said: "Come to me, all of you who are weary and carry heavy burdens, and I will give you rest.*" I was tired and I needed rest. I still liked getting high, but I was tired of the life and all the drama, shame, guilt and disgust that came with it. I really wasn't built for that life anymore. The crack game had used me up and spit me out.

On Sunday morning, February 17, 2010, I walked into Saints Memorial Church after coming off one of my all-night cocaine crack binges. Even though my crack habit was off the chain and I was a complete mess, it didn't stop me from going to church this particular Sunday. I had made a promise to a relative that I wanted to keep. My mother told me church was the best place to be, whether you are saved or unsaved. However, just going to church was not enough to get me delivered. I had some real demons that were not leaving me without a fight. But I hoped the Word of God would prick my heart, speak to my spirit and transform my life. However, I had to do the work. And until I submitted myself to the will of God and made a conscious effort to alter my life, nothing was going to change. That's easier said than done, especially when your will and desire to get high has controlled you for nearly your whole life.

The day before, on Saturday, February 16, 2010, I had seen some of my family at a baby shower. My mother's sister, Aunt Mary, was there. I was glad to see her even though things were not so good between us. She had stopped talking to me and I didn't know exactly why. I'm sure it had something to do with the drugs. I really missed her. I was willing to do anything to rebuild the relationship we once had. It might sound corny, but I wanted her love back. Crackheads need love too. I told her I was coming to church the next day. She was glad. I was hoping that by going to church I could connect with her again and maybe even get delivered in the process.

My drug use invited all kinds of demonic spirits to have complete sovereignty in my life. It has destroyed so many relationships that I once valued. However, I lived to get high and was powerless to stop. Yet deep down in my soul I wanted to quit. More than that, I needed to change because death and eternal damnation was calling me. I was stuck in a psychotic paradox of wanting to be delivered, while at the same time constantly bombarded with urges to get high. It was a vicious cycle that was never ending. The Apostle

Paul said, *"When I would do good evil is always present."* I loved God and I loved getting high. How is that possible? To most people that probably sounds like insanity and for many years of my life it was. There was a constant battle in my mind and spirit. I had two dueling forces fighting for my love and loyalty and I couldn't pick the right one. The Word of God says: *"No one can serve two masters. Either you will hate the one and love the other, or you will be devoted to the one and despise the other."* Crack cocaine will only accept first place in your life. It will cause you to abandon or destroy anything else that tries to replace it. But buried deep down inside of me was a "Yes" for God. Beneath all the drugs, dysfunction and trauma was a small piece of my spirit that was screaming "Yes, God." The enemy did everything it could to choke my "Yes" but he didn't have the power. Whether I accepted it or not, God had chosen me. So even when I had given up, God didn't let that "Yes" die.

Saints Memorial church was familiar to me. A lot of my relatives, including my aunt, were members of the ministry. My mother was married to the founder and she helped plant the church. Even though she had a strategic part in its development, it was never really a happy or peaceful place to me. There wasn't anything specific about it that really bothered me, I just never felt completely comfortable. Growing up in different churches throughout my life, I know there is no perfect church. Every church has its gossipers, backbiters and cliques. I didn't really care about any of that stuff. As long as the Lord is present in the church, you can still find deliverance. That's why I was there, hoping and wishing that I could get delivered. However, for true deliverance I needed to do more than hope and wish. I had the responsibility to fight for my deliverance. The enemy wasn't going to just flee without a fight. That morning the worship service was blessed. The Spirit of the Lord was moving in the congregation. I could feel the presence of the Lord all over my body and sensed something was going to occur. As the Spirit of the Lord began to work in my heart and soul, tears began to stream down my face. I cried out to the Lord to save me from me and the life I was living. In the Book of Romans the Word of God says: *"That if thou shalt confess with thy mouth the Lord Jesus, and shalt believe in thine heart that God hath raised Him from the dead, thou shalt be saved."*

At the end of the service, they had an altar call. I walked to the front of the church and gave my life to the Lord. In that moment I was saved. The Bible says that if any man be in Jesus he is a new creation. I was a new creation but the devil tried to convince me I wasn't. So here I was a brand new creature with an old crack pipe in my mouth, getting high the same night I gave my life to the Lord. There was nothing new about that. The enemy was laughing at me. I was stuck because the taste of drugs was vicious and would not leave my mouth. And to keep it all the way real, especially to those who struggle with addiction, I still loved getting high.

For some "religious, churchy" people who are not nearly as enlightened as they profess, my confession is really difficult for them to digest. They ask, "How can God be on the inside and you still be addicted to illicit drugs?" My reply is: "The same way as whoremongers, liars, fornicators and every other sinner that walks the earth and claims God on the inside." We all have sinned and come short of His Glory. It's time to stop compartmentalizing and categorizing sins. There are no big sins and little sins. Sin is sin in the eyes of God. For far too long, we as Christians have been taught in error about how the Spirit of God works. A lot of the teachings Christians receive is based on denominational folklore that has been passed down generations. Some of it is used to keep people in line and suppress spiritual development of lay members and is really about control. No group or denomination can define how God is supposed to deliver people. I read God is no respecter of persons. What He does for one, He can do for all. There is a process all of us must go through when we come to Christ. And just like we all have a personal relationship with the Lord, we also have a personal deliverance with Him as well. It only makes sense because we all come to him with our own set of baggage. Still, the idea of me continuing to get high and claim salvation at the same time was a tough pill for church people to swallow. Partly because so many church people, when they witness, tell you that once you accept Christ in your life and into your heart you are immediately transformed, healed and delivered. As you grow in grace, you will soon see that those beliefs passed down were simply fallacies. All you have to do is spend a little time reading the Bible and you will see that Jesus healed and delivered in many ways. Sometimes He healed with one touch and sometimes He healed with multiple touches. Then sometimes He didn't heal at all and let the believer know that His grace is sufficient in their life.

Now in my case, I knew what I was doing was wrong and contrary to the will of God. Every time I did it I felt more and more guilty. Going to church high on drugs I felt shameful. However, one day I was watching the Trinity Broadcast Network (TBN). I heard the preacher quote 1 John 1:9: *"If we confess our sins, He is faithful and righteous to forgive us our sins and to cleanse us from all unrighteousness."* Something kicked in. That scripture gave me hope and direction. True repentance had begun. I was constantly confessing my sins before Jesus. And I had plenty to confess. Gradually things began to change in my life. I started to hate getting high. Each time was less and less fulfilling and more demoralizing, causing me to feel more worthless. I wanted to live saved and in the perfect will of God. I wanted to be completely delivered, but things seemed to get worse. It was a major struggle.

On May 29th of that same year, I had a date with destiny. I went to church and something happened.

Service was great. It was the second service of the day. I didn't make the first one because I was out getting high. Anyways, we were celebrating the First Lady of the church. The church had brought in a guest speaker on that night and she was a powerful woman of God. It started when one of the leaders of the church, who was also one of my mother's best friends, looked at me and asked if I was tired and ready to surrender. Of course I was, but I was ready every other time I went to church too. But I was this time, and I told her "Yes." That "Yes" I had for God was breaking its way through. In the midst of the guest speaker preaching, she stopped mid-sentence and pointed to me and said, "Today the Lord is going to deliver you." I don't know if I completely believed her at the time because I had heard it hundred times before. People prophesied to me, my mother and my family about how God was going to deliver me, but it hadn't come to pass. I was hopeful this night. I was focused, praising and worshipping the Lord with all my heart. With tears rolling, arms flailing in praise, I was confessing and asking God for complete deliverance. After the message, she made an altar call and I walked up. She laid hands on me, but I didn't feel a difference. She was determined and so was I. She told me, "God said you are going to be delivered today." I walked back to my seat and sat down. She said "no come back" and she prayed again and laid hands on me. That time, I felt everything leave my body, including the crack I had smoked just before service. The more than 30 year taste of crack and illegal drugs was completely removed from me. That demonic spirit was cast out of me. God's "Yes" had broken through all the mess. It was the greatest day of my life. The only thing missing was my mom. Although she had gone on to Glory, she laid the foundation for my deliverance with her years of prayers, fasting and petitioning of the Lord. I knew the Lord had moved in my life but I wasn't exactly sure what deliverance meant. The only way to know if I was really, truly delivered would be my ability to resist. Two weeks later, one of my old get high partners called and asked me for $20 for food. I knew it was game right away. I told her "I'm not giving you $20. What do you want? I'll buy it. I'm heading to church but I'll bring you some food on my way." I had used that "food game" a hundred times. I'm saved, not a sucker. I picked up the food for her and brought it over. I probably shouldn't have gone over there because it was a crack house. I had spent many years there getting high and doing all kinds of things. When I got to the house, I knocked on the door and they opened it. There were crackheads everywhere. Everyone was smoking crack, and it seemed like they all collectively blew the smoke in my face. Normally I wouldn't have been able to handle that, but this time I was not affected. I started thanking and praising God right there at the crack house door with the crackheads peering. I let them all know, "God did this! He delivered me! All of you need is Jesus!" I left praising God. I was set free. The feelings of exhilaration were incredible but feelings only last for so long. When you come off that cloud, you have to step back into a real world with real problems.

Chapter Twenty-One

"But I say, walk by the Spirit, and you
will not gratify the desires of the flesh."
Galatians 5:16

I'm saved—now what? For most of my life I lived a crazy, crack-cocaine filled existence. Smoking crack, tricking and pulling stunts was a normal day for me. I really didn't know how to do anything else. What was I going to do now, go start working a 9 to 5 in some corporate office downtown? I can't imagine myself sitting in a cubicle for eight hours, trying to focus on something I have no desire to do. Maybe I could turn into the perfect housewife? For so long I had been living in an underworld of society that was completely different from the real world. I thought once I was delivered everything would be all good. That's what they kept telling me in church. Get saved and everything will be all better. But life is not fair and living saved is not easy. I was delivered but I had a ton of baggage and a lot of growing to do. I was severely damaged. I was 53 years old but I had stopped maturing emotionally around the age of 23, the week I started freebasing. The world had gone on and I had to try and catch up. I couldn't hide from the world and just wait for God to fix my life. He didn't mess it up, I did. So now I had to go fix it. I had to face the world and start to work on me. If I didn't fix me I wouldn't be any help to anyone else.

One of my biggest challenges was learning how to be a Godly wife to my current husband, Glyne. Since I had given my life to the Lord, it was my responsibility to live according to His will. That meant following His instructions in every area of my life. That also meant submitting myself to an unsaved man that I didn't have a whole lot of respect for. We were no match made in heaven and we were far from soul mates. We really had only two things in common and they were "getting high" and "tricking," both of those areas we mastered. He never showed any affection. Well at least not the kind that I was accustomed to. He wasn't a touchy, feely guy and he wasn't going to tell me I was special or beautiful. His idea of affection was giving me money. It was a cultural norm that I learned to accept. That's the man who was the head of my house, and the one I was supposed to look to for guidance. My husband and I had a lot of history and the majority of it was dysfunctional. Even though I had been off and on with Glyne since 1989, we never had a real relationship where both of us were clean from drugs. I met him after another one of my failed relationships. Chester and I were finally over for real. I moved out of the apartment never to return again. He had gotten to be too ridiculous and I was done with him. My addiction was out of control and had elevated to another level. When you are smoking crack like I was, you just keep sinking to new lows. Things never get any better, they only get worse. And the awful and disgusting things you subject yourself to often have a negative effect on the people closest to you. Back then, I changed men like people change underwear. I always had more than one man in my life. I just learned how to manipulate and manage them all. As soon as I got my new apartment, I was right back on my grind. I started tricking with some of the young, neighborhood drug dealers. Most of them were not much older than my son. I had a lot of experience so they were turned on by my sexual abilities. Those young boys had never been a real woman, especially one who made a living selling her body. At the same time I was out doing my thing, my son was messing around in the streets hanging with the wrong crowd. There wasn't much I could really say to him. It wasn't like me or his father were great role models. When you have two crackheads for parents, you are pretty much on your own. As a result, what happened to him is what happens to everybody who chooses a life of crime. They say it is either jail or the grave. One day he was arrested for stealing a car and ended up in Nashua Street Jail. At least it was not the grave. While inside, he met some drug dealers from around our way. They were in the jail's rec room talking. A couple of the guys started telling him about some new lady that moved around their way. They said she was a crackhead that gave good head and great sex. He realized they were talking about me, his mother. He was so embarrassed that he refused to come live with me when he got out. When they released him from jail, he went to live with Chester, the guy who I had just gotten away from. That's pretty bad when your own son would rather live with your ex, who is not even his real father, than live with you. He stayed with Chester until he hustled up enough money to go live with his biological father. But I can't blame him. That whole conversation had to be pretty humiliating. It still didn't stop me. I was running hard smoking like a deranged person.

When I met my husband, Glyne, he was at a neighbor's crack house getting high. Glyne was what you would call a functional crackhead. He had a profession and worked in the construction industry. He tricked hard and worked hard too. Glyne always had two things, money and cocaine. We were attracted to each other so I got with him one day and took him to my house. We were getting real high and I was all over him. But he was kind of a shy person and I think I was too aggressive for him. That's part of his culture. So while we were getting high, he told me he was going to buy some more drugs and he would be right back. He never came back. I wasn't mad at him for running out on me, that was part of the life. I moved out of the area and we fell out of contact. I never saw him again until I went to my neighbor's house and there he was. This time he was with his woman, Faith, and they were hanging tough. So I fell back. A couple years later we met up again and he was still with Faith. I tried to be respectful of their relationship, but in the lifestyle we were living, respect is easily compromised. So one day my cousin came around telling me about some guy that was coming to the crack house to spend some serious money. I needed a come up, so I went up there with my cousin. When we got upstairs in the crack house, there was Glyne and some other dude I had never seen before. I was happy to see Glyne, it had been a minute. I went right over and sat with him. My cousin stated, "That ain't the guy, the other guy is the one spending the money." I told him that I didn't care about the other guy; I wanted to be with Glyne. Glyne and I started talking and hanging out. We ended up sleeping together that night. We tried to get together but things faded out quickly. I guess it still wasn't our time. Nearly 10 years later Glyne and I reconnected. I started going to his house, but I had to be cool because he was still with Faith, however they were on shaky ground. I spent a lot time getting high at his house; and I would go off with different men and Glyne would get very upset. But he was tricking with everybody except me. About a year later, Glyne's lady had a stroke. They were already on shaky ground so they broke up shortly after that. So I had to make him see that I was the best choice. I seized my opportunity. A lot of women were chasing Glyne because he had money. My mother told me if you want to get a man you have to be a woman to him. So I did just that. I played the role of wife and did all the cooking, cleaning and washing. While I was trying to get him, I didn't even get high. He was going to be, mine and I wasn't going to let any of them get him. My plan worked and all the other women were gone. I got him, but my mother told me things were not going to be great between us. She said he was too old for me and our cultural differences would drive a wedge in our relationship. I didn't know what she was talking about. Honestly, I paid her no mind. I believed I could make it work with my new hero. As usual, she was right. Our cultural differences were blinding; yet, I couldn't really see them. Maybe I just chose to ignore them because I wanted to be with him. One day I thought things were going along fine and we were lying in bed and I passed gas. Glyne got so furious with me. It was a natural thing and I didn't do it on purpose. Why was he so angry? In his eyes, I had disrespected him. And women should never disrespect men. That was one of those cultural differences my mother warned me about. He started calling me all kinds of nasty names and punched me in the head. I couldn't believe it. I was hurt. I wasn't trying to disrespect him. I loved him. At that time, I was trying to do everything I could to make him happy. But here I was, yet again, in another abusive, dysfunctional relationship. I left Glyne's house and went to stay at my mother's. I wasn't going to deal with being hit again. He called me and said sorry. He asked me to come back home with him. He assured me that it would not happen again. That was the extent of his apology. He wanted me back, but he wasn't going to beg me or even ask me too many times. His pride wouldn't allow it. In his eyes, that was the best he could do. I guess he was remorseful, as remorseful as a staunch West Indian man could be. But really, what abuser have you ever heard of that stops after the first time. Still, I agreed to go home. When he came to pick me up, my mother confronted him. She said, "Son, you can't be putting your hands on my *Puncho*. Don't do it again or she is coming back here to stay with me." Here I was, in my 40's and my mother was still watching over and protecting me. She loved my husband but wasn't going to let any man hurt me. The hitting did stop for a while. But eventually the abuse started up again. Glyne put his hands on me a few more times, but I started to fight back. I think I just accepted hitting as being part of a relationship. It reverts back to my childhood where I witnessed men beat women and believed that was how they showed their love. Repeated dysfunction turns into normal behavior. So I think it just became normal to me and something I could live with. Because I still wanted to try and make it work, we decided to get married. We went down and got our blood tests, then went down to the courthouse and got our marriage license. After that, I went to my mother and asked her if she would marry us. She refused and said our marriage would never work. She said: "How in the world are two drug addicts going to get married, plus I told you he was too old for you. West Indian men are different from American men.

They have major cultural differences. Did you forget he knocked you upside your head for farting in the bed? I didn't, and I won't marry you." So I went ahead and asked another pastor to marry us. This pastor was all too willing to marry us. She was from the "It's better to marry than to burn" school. However, there were all kinds of red flags I didn't see that were right in my face. I was high on crack the day of my marriage. We were all dressed in black for a wedding celebration. Those were major flags that I didn't pick up on until I was clean and sober and had a clear head. Now I know a lot of women get married and think because of the ceremony things will get better, usually they don't. People don't change unless God transforms them. Glyne was no different. About a year later, my mother went home to be with the Lord and everything that she said about my marriage turned out to be true.

Now living as a saved woman, I have to reap what I've sowed. I have to honor a marriage which started out dishonorably. I have to respect a man that doesn't honor me, and I have to do it with integrity. That's a tough assignment because while I'm fighting to maintain my deliverance, I still had to endure physical, verbal and emotional abuse from my husband. I needed to somehow obtain my respect and dignity in the home. I was Glyne's wife, but also God's child. Glyne didn't care that I had stopped using drugs and gave my life to the Lord. He still saw the same strung out Bethann that he married 10 years ago. He didn't understand salvation. He didn't understand his wife was a new creature. To him, I was the same woman he met tricking in the crack house. And every chance he had, he would let me know what he thought about me. A couple of times Glyne spoke to me disrespectfully in front of clients saying things no man should ever say to a woman, never mind a husband to his wife. A couple of times we had knockdown, drag- out fights. It was a roller coaster ride. Once, we even got into a physical fight in a moving car where I knocked out a few of his teeth. Yes, I did. He was disrespecting my son, and I lost it for a minute. I got it together, and he will never disrespect my son again. It took a few years for us to finally arrive at a place of understanding. We're cordial with each other, however, we live more like roommates than husband and wife. There is no intimacy, just mutual respect. Still a far cry away from the hero I always dreamed of marrying.

Chapter Twenty-Two

"The one who has knowledge uses words with restraint,
and whoever has understanding is even-tempered."
Proverbs 17:27

Not only did I have to adjust to my new life in my home, I also had to make adjustments in the street. This has been an ongoing process. It hasn't been easy and every now and then something or someone attempts to throw me off. If I'm not prayerful, I may react in a way that's not so holy. I'm saved, but I haven't forgotten how to fight and protect myself nor have I forgotten how to tell someone off either. I am still growing in grace when it comes to my mouth. Over the last few years, I have worked hard to keep myself away from toxic situations and my tongue under subjection. Proverbs 18:21 says, *"Death and life are in the power of the tongue."*

I'm delivered beyond the shadow, but the demons of my past life are still ever before me trying to destroy my bond with Jesus. I am constantly in spiritual warfare. The demons of my past hate the new me because they know whose side I am on. I don't feel the need to carry around a sign that says I'm with God. I wear it in my heart and demonstrate it by the life I lead. Those who know the old Bethann know I'm a changed person. Still, some people refuse to acknowledge the transformation. I won't call them haters, even though that's what they are. They prefer the old Bethann. Other folks are determined to make me pay for the sins of my past life; but that's too bad for them. God forgave me and threw my sins into the proverbial sea of forgetfulness. My debt has been paid. However, every now and then someone tries to collect on an old debt. As recent as two years ago, I started getting threatening calls from an old acquaintance. We used to run the streets hard. We ran all kinds of flimflams and tricked together many times. But that was more than 10 years ago and before I gave me life to the Lord. My guess is that Stacy must have been feigning for crack and scheming on ways to get money. She must have been really desperate. That's the only reason she would be crazy enough to call my phone with some nonsense. Desperation will make you do crazy things. It's part of the sickness. I've been at that place before in my life, but she wasn't about to get a come up off of me.

She went into some old story about the time I beat her for two eight balls of cocaine. I remember the situation as clear as day. I played her, but that was part of the game. She was really forcing it. She started threatening to expose me to the church. I had already confessed all of my dirty secrets and released my skeletons. My life was an open book and I told on myself. So I told her to do what she needed to do. When she didn't get the response she wanted, she threatened me with bodily harm. The funny part about her threats was the fact that she knew she couldn't whoop me. She wasn't built like that. She was not a fighter. I knew it was all talk, but I still wanted to address her threats. Honestly, I wanted to check her and let her know that just because I was saved, didn't mean she couldn't get her behind beat. Jesus saved and delivered me from drugs and lust, not fighting. I still knew how to do that. I actually drove over to Stacy's home to confront her. She thought because I was no longer ripping and running in the streets I was off my game and she'd catch me slippin. Nah Boo Boo, nice try though! I sat outside her house for a minute, and then the Lord rebuked me and I pulled off and went back home. I'm so glad that nothing actually transpired between us. I'm a living testimony to the healing and deliverance power of God. While beating her butt for what she tried might have felt good for a moment, I would have felt bad afterwards. Bad that I let God down and I let her down, knowing she needs Jesus. I pray that Stacy gets delivered and finds hope in God. Stacy wasn't the only person in their feelings about past dealings. There were many others looking to settle the score with me; people wanting to hurt me for what I did to them. I had to deal with the damage I caused, which was tremendous, while learning to live saved at the same time. It wasn't easy. Just walking down the street some days was a challenge. Seeing people I slept with to get drugs sometimes made me sick to my stomach. I can't believe I allowed myself to stoop that low. But it wasn't me, it was the addiction. Some of those people would say the meanest and nastiest things to me just because they knew I was saved. They would bring up sexual acts I performed on them or let them perform on me and laugh, reminding me how disgusting I was. It was so humiliating. Some days I didn't even want to leave the house. But I couldn't hide from my past. I had to confront it. However, because I knew so many people, it seemed like it was a constant battle and I never knew when things would pop off. So, I just walked around prepared.

Boston is such a small city and I knew one day I would bump into Dre. Dre was a neighborhood drug dealer who had a reputation of hurting people who crossed him. I heard some bad stories in the past about him. He was known for taking "no shorts," which meant you had to have the full amount of money when you went to cop some crack from him. But back in the day when I was copping from Dre, I was a savage with a crazy habit. I had a million and one ways to get money and that made me one of his best customers. My hustle game was incredible and it gave me favor with Dre and other local dealers. They would front me drugs because they were confident I would be back at some point. Many of them knew my husband, Glyne. They knew the type of work he did and the type of money he made and figured if I played them, they would get the money from him. But at the end of my run, I burnt every bridge and Dre wasn't the only dealer pissed off at me. Some of those people were livid and wanted my blood. I had an answering machine full of threats from both men and women. A few of them said they were going to shoot me. Others said they would have me ganged raped and record it. Talk about sick, perverted people. They were willing to do anything to get revenge on me for beating them.

The last time I saw Dre he fronted me some cocaine and I never went back to pay him. To keep it all the way real, I felt like it was his fault. At the end of the day can you really trust a crackhead to keep their word? Dre knew I was strung out and he should have expected one of those times I wouldn't come back with his money. Nowadays, they call it "running off on the plug." But back then it was just beating the dealer. And during my more than 30 years on the streets, I beat a lot of dealers. Anyways, it had been a number of years since we last saw each other. Dre had a memory like an elephant and no way he'd forgotten my debt. Besides, no drug dealers or drug addicts ever forget the time they got beat for money or product, no matter how large or small the amount. So I sort of figured he would be upset when we finally crossed paths. Sure enough, one afternoon when I got off the bus to go do some grocery shopping, there he was, Dre in the flesh. He angrily approached me, but I wasn't afraid. However, I didn't expect the first thing to come out of his mouth to be, "Where is my money, trick?" Initially, I was upset at his disrespect. Those were fighting words. If I hadn't been delivered, I probably would have swung on him. But that violent street behavior was part of the old, unforgiven and un-redeemed me. I had given up every aspect of that life and hadn't turned tricks or been in a fight in years. Besides, Dre had been slanging long enough to know everybody takes losses in the streets. There is an unwritten rule "chalk it up to the game." However, on that day this dude was in his feelings and felt the need to be extra disrespectful. Lucky for him he was dealing with this new version of Bethann who was saved and delivered.

But I was on the verge of cursing him out if he kept going. Instead, I kept my mouth under subjection, remained cool and walked off with my integrity. I lived that crazy drug life for so many years that I understood his anger. I had been beaten on drug deals many times in my life and none of them ever felt good. As crazy as it sounds, on some level I empathized with him. However I wasn't paying him back and I guess my response didn't help, especially considering how dangerous he was. When the Lord saved me, He gave me holy boldness. I looked Dre right in his eyes and told him he wasn't getting one thin dime from me. I told him I was delivered from my old life and any issues he had with me, he needed to take it up with God. I'm sure that probably sounded crazy to a sinner like him, but that was my reality. I didn't feel bad at all because we had an illegal and unholy relationship that kept me strung out, while preparing me for an early grave. There was no honor or integrity in our dealings. Back then, I was a crackhead and he was a drug dealer and in that game people got beat every day.

Now there were past relationships that the Holy Spirit advised me to address. In some cases, I needed to apologize and make amends and even restitution.

But Dre and my relationship wasn't one of those times. In one swoop, the Holy Spirit ended our dealer-addict relationship along with my love and desire of the whole sinful world. God plucked me out of that world of bondage. All the dirt, games, crime and trickery of my past life was dead and gone. All the debts, shady deals and tricks were cancelled. I believe the Lord brought me back to the place where it all started to show His power and might. He allowed me to live in the same area where I ran the streets for years to show forth His Glory. I see a lot of the old crowd I used to get high with and commit crimes. Many of them can't believe that I have been delivered and redeemed. A lot of them are blown away by my new life and my zeal to spread the gospel of Jesus Christ. However, some are dying for the day I relapse.

Chapter Twenty-Three

*"Therefore, if anyone is in Christ, he is a
new creation. The old has passed away.
Behold, the new has come."*
2 Corinthians 5:17

This new life was not easy to figure out at all. Besides adjusting to my home life and dealing with people in the streets, I had to learn how society operated. I was almost like an immigrant from a foreign country coming to live here in America. For 30 years I lived in the demonic, crack underworld. I lived to get high. What was normal for me would be psychotic to the average person. I missed years at a time in the real world. I was oblivious to changes, inventions and advancements. So many things happened in the world that I missed out on.

I remember once being on a month long binge and waking up out of a haze on my brother's couch. He was a big time drug dealer at the time and had all kinds of gadgets at his house. Anyways, I looked up at his TV and this funny looking machine that looked like it was something from the space age was on top of it. It was a DVD player. I had no clue what it was and no idea how long this thing had been out. The last thing I remembered was a VCR, which I sold for some crack. It may seem silly but it's true. When you are really getting high like I was, your whole life is consumed with the chase for the next hit. Everything else, unless it's a means to getting more drugs, does not concern you. So, even my communication skills had to develop. I had to learn the lingo or I would be out of touch. I would end up being the square trying to figure out the game. A lot of words and sayings had double meanings that I wasn't even aware of.

For instance, back in the day flirting and courting was much different than it is today. Back then, if you were out at the mall or the movies or the nightclub or just walking down the street and you met someone that you were interested in, you would ask for their telephone number. We didn't have email yet and there was no Facebook or other social media platforms to connect with people. The only way to really communicate with the person you were interested in was by telephone. Often times when we asked for phone numbers, we didn't always include the word "telephone" before number; we would just shorten it and say, "What's your number?" If someone asked for your number and you were not interested in them, you would tell them to step-off or else you would give them a fake number. I gave out my share of fake numbers, especially when the dudes were trying too hard. But when you were really interested in someone, you would give them your real number and hopefully some kind of relationship would evolve.

Nowadays things are totally different. There are a million ways to connect with people. And things that once meant one thing years ago, now mean something else. For instance, today when someone asks, "What's your number?" they are usually not talking about your telephone number. Instead, they are inquiring about something much more personal and private. They are talking about the number of people with whom you have had sexual relations. They want to know what the streets call "your body count." To most people, whether fairly or unfairly, that number determines what kind of person you are. A low number usually means you are on the conservative side and possible boyfriend/girlfriend material. A higher number means you like to get your "freak on" or you are what the young people call a "Thot." Just know the higher the number the freakier people assume you are. Usually the higher number people are not looking for a relationship but rather a cheap thrill or good time. Your number can absolutely be a deal breaker, especially when considering entering into a relationship with someone. I don't know too many people that want a partner with a high number. Thank God Jesus doesn't care about our number. He loves us unconditionally and in spite of our worldly numbers.

Anyways, I'm a married woman and I've been off-the-market for a long time so no man has the right to ask me my number. And if any man had the nerve to ask me, I would not even dignify them with a response. But, now hypothetically speaking, if I was single and came across a man I was interested in having a relationship with and he asked me that question, it would be a different story. I would tell him my number, but he'd probably run away as fast as he could when he heard it. I'm a keep it real type of person. I speak my truth and you can hear it throughout the pages of this book. My truth is serious and incredibly staggering. There are not too many people who would be able to handle the truth when it comes to my real number. It would lead to serious judgement. It's one of the hardest parts of my personal testimony. When I reflect on the more than 30 years I hustled as a prostitute on the mean, dirty streets of Boston, so many nasty images flash before me. During that time I know I must have had sex with hundreds of men and women. That's right I said "hundreds" and only one third of the time we used protection. It's crazy to hear myself say it aloud so I can only imagine what someone reading this book thinks. But that is the reality of the life I used to live. As a crack fiend, prostituting was the primary way I made money to support my habit. There is an endless supply of johns aka tricks, willing to spend money for a quick sexual thrill with no thought of the consequences. A lot of people call it a victimless crime, but I bet they never worked the streets I worked because if they did they would see the victimization that takes place on a daily basis. It was a thrill for the tricks, but it was a job for me. It is a dirty business and each encounter takes something from you. The world has a saying that many people live by which is, "Whatever doesn't kill you makes you stronger." There is some truth to that theory. However, I live by a different theory. I operate in the Kingdom of God. And in the Kingdom of God, His Grace along with my favorite set of twins, "Goodness and Mercy," protect and preserve me.

Addiction is so powerful that it causes you to do things you would never do in your right mind, and sleep with people whom disgust you and people you would never even associate with if you were not getting high. Those types of people make up 99% of my number. What's worse is that many of them were not only nasty, they were infected with all kinds of STD's including HIV and AIDS. I was blessed not to have contracted HIV. But I didn't come out completely unscathed because I contracted other things like gonorrhea and chlamydia. Those are just a few of the consequences that came with the life. Thanks be to God that I'm cured from all those diseases and instead of being some strung out, crackhead statistic, infected with all kinds of sicknesses, I am saved, sanctified, sanitized and spotless. I know some of you reading this are probably saying "spotless?" How in the devil does she have the audacity to say spotless? Well, He redeemed me and I'm in His will. And because I'm in his Perfect Will, I follow the instructions Paul wrote in Philippians *2:14-15: "Do everything without grumbling or arguing, so that you may become blameless and spotless, "children of God without fault in a warped and crooked generation." Then you will shine among them like stars in the sky."*

Addiction is powerful, but the blood of Jesus is much more powerful. I have been blood-washed. And while numbers don't lie, Jesus has the final say. There is only one number that truly matters in my life now and that is the number three, and it represents the Holy Trinity which is the Father, Son and Holy Ghost. So to all my brothers and sisters, when you are asked for your number, if you have been born again tell them "three."

Chapter Twenty-Four

*"We must let go of the life we have
planned, so as to accept the one that
is waiting for us."*
Joseph Campbell

Sometimes it seems as though life was easier when I was getting high, as crazy as that sounds. That's probably because I was always under the influence of some kind of drug and didn't feel much pain. Back then, when I was overwhelmed, I could just get a blast of crack and all of those feelings would go away for a while. But that was the old me. I don't have crack or any magic pill to help me escape from the pain. Sitting on my couch, looking out the window with nothing but time on my hands, my mind would run a million miles an hour. I was dealing with multiple situations in my mind. I had my relationship with my husband, Glyne. I had all the guilt and shame associated with my son who is sitting in prison with the possibility of never coming home for something he didn't even do. I also had the memories of my mother and the shame and guilt I felt for not being there for her in her final days. I was also working to reconcile with my estranged family. Then I had all the people who were determined to make me curse God and go back to smoking again. With so much guilt, shame and anxiety, I just wanted to crawl up like a little ball in the corner.

I'm saved. This is supposed to be the best time of my life. I'm not supposed to feel worthless. I am now a child of the King. I have been forgiven and justified. But then again, they say the devil doesn't bother you when you are not saved because he already has you. It's when you openly declare your allegiance to Jesus Christ that the adversary comes seeking to devour you. He was definitely coming for me with an army of imps. I had to be ready for the battle. The more I prayed, the more the Lord would speak to me. Each day I got a little stronger. The Lord inspired me to work on my ministry. He had given me the idea of a television broadcast. He even gave me the name. Things were actually going pretty well. I was getting ready for my first television broadcast when I got a call from a friend. She told me to look on Facebook, there were some very compromising videos of me. I logged on and watched them in horror. There were multiple video clips of me performing sexual acts on men and women. I was devastated. An angry drug dealer had posted the videos. I was so embarrassed and humiliated. I told the executive producer of the show that I was sick and couldn't do the broadcast. It was true, I was sick. I was sick to my stomach. Their ploy worked that day. I even considered not doing the broadcast ever again. But the Lord strengthened me. I got it together and my broadcast has been going strong now for almost eight years. The broadcast had some bumps along the way. A few times I connected with people who were not whom they professed to be. However, the Spirit revealed their true identity as well as their motives. Some of them were close to me, but wrong is wrong and sin is sin no matter who it is.

Chapter Twenty-Five

"For if we would judge ourselves,
We should not be judged."
1 Corinthians 11:31

"One of my biggest accomplishments since giving my life to the Lord is the self-awareness I have gained. It took me a while to develop it over the last ten years, given the amount of drugs I consumed. After 30 plus years of abusing crack cocaine and other hard drugs, sometimes my brain is like scrambled eggs. I have a million thoughts swimming around in my head. Nevertheless, for the most part I am able to think straight. I'm constantly working to become a better person. The Bible says,

"Let a man examine himself." I have done a lot of self-examining and came to the realization that I accumulated a lot of baggage over the years. And if I don't manage my baggage, I can be a problem to those trying to deal with me. Being saved doesn't mean I have arrived, it just means I have been redeemed. I have bad days just like everyone else. I still have character flaws and traits that I have to work on. I'm a control freak and I know it. I can be rough and abrasive. And sometimes I just say what's on my mind without considering the consequences. At times my realness or bluntness offends people. Some are threatened by my deliverance and anointing. Others resent the fact that I lived the life I used to live and now I am richly blessed. I'm the prodigal daughter who has come home to my Father God. He has shown me favor. Yes, me, the former crackhead. Favor isn't fair and it is not reserved just for those who go to church all the time and do the right thing. It's also for the whosoevers, which includes prostitutes, criminals, drug abusing crackheads and any others who have come short of God's Word. Jealous people and the enemy hate that God works like that. One thing that is

important for all believers to understand is that although you may have been saved and delivered for several years, the enemy will not rest until he has you back. He wants you under his control and out of the will and favor of God. I see it every day. There is not a day that goes by where the enemy does not try to tempt me. Some temptations will look like pure evil and they are easy to recognize while others are cleverly disguised. Some attacks will come at you in subtle ways that appear non-threatening and harmless. Their suggestions may be reasonable, but they may be laying a trap. If the enemy can get you to let your guard down and compromise your integrity just a little bit, then he has sown corruptible seeds of destruction in your life. A lot of times, sin starts off feeling good and masks itself as innocence. We have to be responsible and disciplined enough to recognize the works of the enemy. I have also worked to develop patience. Some things in life we just have to go through. The hardest thing sometimes is waiting for God to release us or deliver us from a situation that we know is unhealthy. So many times during my active addiction period I did what I wanted and felt I needed to do to get a fix. My behavior was calculated. I constantly planned and plotted about how to get my next fix. No one or nothing would keep me from getting high. So now my life is completely different and I work diligently to make no moves until I hear from the Lord. And by that, I don't mean the Lord is talking to me for hours at a time every day. Through my prayer life and the study of His Word is how I now navigate through life. Then when temptations arise, I bring them to Him openly and honestly. I ask the Lord to help with them so I don't make poor decisions or fall out of His will. Because the Lord knew I would need comfort in my walk with Him, He sent me a comforter which is the Holy Spirit. John said of this spirit: *"When he, the Spirit of truth, is come, he will guide you into all truth: for he shall not speak of himself; but whatsoever he shall hear, that shall he speak: and he will shew you things to come"*.

The Holy Ghost has kept me these last ten years and I thank God.

Chapter Twenty-Six

*"Arise, shine, for your light has come, and
the glory of the Lord has risen upon you."*
Isaiah 60:1

Whe everything was all said and done, after thousands of schemes, after all the abuse and dysfunction and after my constant quest to find Mr. Right and having to settle for Mr. Right now, who eventually turned into Mr. Wrong, I realized that the hero I spent most of my life searching for was right there, bidding me to come. He kept knocking at the door of my heart waiting for me to invite Him in. He was more faithful to me than any man had ever been. No matter how low I sank, He never left my side.

When the Angel of death sent drugs, bullets and diseases to try and destroy me, my Hero covered me in His Blood. He dispatched angels, like Michael and Gabriel, to fight on my behalf. His name is Jesus and He is my one true Hero. Not only is He my Hero, He is also my Friend. No human can ever take His place. Nothing can separate me from His love, for it is from everlasting to everlasting.

I pray you find hope in the true and living Jesus and you allow Him to be your Hero.